EXPERIMENTAL PSYCHOLOGY:

A COMPUTERIZED LABORATORY COURSE

EXPERIMENTAL PSYCHOLOGY:

A COMPUTERIZED LABORATORY COURSE

J.T. MULLIN AND I.W.R. BUSHNELL

University Of Glasgow

LAWRENCE ERLBAUM ASSOCIATES, PUBLISHERS
London   Hillsdale, New Jersey

Copyright © 1987 by Lawrence Erlbaum Associates Ltd.
  All rights reserved. No part of this book may be reproduced in
any form, by photostat, microform, retrieval system, or any
other means without the prior written permission of the
publisher.

Lawrence Erlbaum Associates Ltd., Publishers
27 Palmeira Mansions
Church Road
Hove
East Sussex BN3 2FA
U.K.

ISBN 0-86377-058-4

Printed and bound by Antony Rowe Ltd.

CONTENTS

Introduction I/1 - I/2

Computer Usage CU/1 - CU/5

Experimental Report Writing ERW/1 - ERW/5

Sample Report SR/1 - SR/7

Chapter 1:   Simple Reaction Time 1/1 - 1/6

Chapter 2:   Word Frequency and Recognition Speed 2/1 - 2/10

Chapter 3:   Waterfall Effect 3/1 - 3/10

Chapter 4:   Muller-Lyer Illusion 4/1 - 4/10

Chapter 5:   Prisoner's Dilemma 5/1 - 5/10

Chapter 6:   Extra-sensory Perception (ESP) 6/1 - 6/8

Chapter 7:   Mental Imagery I and II 7/1 - 7/14

Chapter 8:   Reading and Selective Attention 8/1 - 8/10

Chapter 9:   Stress, Life Events and Personality Type 9/1 - 9/11

Chapter 10:   Hemispheric Asymmetry I and II 10/1 - 10/16

Chapter 11:   Subliminal Perception 11/1 - 11/12

Glossary G/1 - G/16

Introduction

This chapter will provide some general advice on the most suitable way to make use of this text.

Identification and Work Record
Write your name clearly in ink using large block capitals on the outside back cover of this book. Also write your name legibly in ink in the appropriate place on the last page of the book, titled Work Record. This record allows a summary record to be maintained of the work that you have completed on this course, together with any comments that tutors have made for your guidance. Make sure that this record is kept up-to-date.

Sequence of Experiments
The order in which experiments are printed is the order in which you should complete them. Some experiments relie on previous ones for specific information about experimental design and data analysis. Do not miss any experiments out, unless you have been specifically told to do so by your tutor.

Reading the Units
Please ensure that you read the Introduction to each experimental chapter very carefully before looking at the experimental details in the Methods section. The introductory section is intended to provide sufficient background information for the student to be able to understand the experimental work of the unit within a relevant context. It does not constitute a comprehensive summary of every aspect of the topic area.

Do not read the Discussion section until the experiment has been completed. In a number of the chapters, additional information about the experiments may be obtained from the instructions on the computer screen. Text and computer program are intended to be complementary, neither can be safely ignored.

Testing Subjects
In most units you will be expected to test yourself as a subject. However, in a number of the units, the experiments *will not work* very well if the subject knows the purpose of the study. We therefore advise that you arrange to test someone who is not a member of your class and should therefore know nothing about the experiment. If this is too difficult, then it may be possible to test other people in your class who have not read the relevant chapter, or even to test yourself by reading only the Methods section of the unit before undertaking the experiment.

In several units, you should test at least one volunteer subject, and although you may well find it difficult to obtain subjects outside the class, it is a very useful thing to do as it will teach you about some of the problems of "real research" and help to develop the skills required in dealing with people in a professional manner.

Answering Questions
You will be expected to answer some questions that are contained in the experimental chapters and carry out any required work such as data analysis. Some of the questions may be specific and factual while others may be general and require you to express points of view and discuss research findings. You must complete any required work for each unit within a short time of running the experiment/s, otherwise you will quickly forget a great deal of what you have done. Where appropriate spaces are provided for answers in the units and you should try to confine yourself to the space provided by being concise and using compact handwriting. Additional space is provided at the end of most chapters and you should clearly reference the location of any answers or part answers that overspill to these pages. It would probably help if you drafted your answers to questions or draft reports onto loose-leaf paper before transferring a final copy into this book.

In addition, you may be expected to complete a multiple-choice test on the computer subsequent to carrying out each experiment. Do not attempt to take this test immediately after the experiment. Give yourself time to read the experimental chapter and to do any additional reading that seems appropriate.

References
At the end of each unit there appears a list of all the experiments and articles that are mentioned within the text. In addition, general textbooks for background reading and specifically relevant papers will frequently be suggested. Some of these will usually have to be read if you are to make an adequate job of answering the questions associated

Introduction

with each unit. It is not, however, being suggested that every reference must be read. Some alternatives are often given, particularly for general texts and statistics books, and some references may not be held by your library (although these can usually be obtained through the inter-library loan scheme).

You can expect to get out of your reading an amount that is proportional to the effort you have expended. The particularly motivated student will seek out their own references by referring to reference journals such as Psychological Abstracts and Social Science Citation Index and by browsing through current journals in the appropriate subject area.

Glossary
Many technical terms are highlighted in the text, being printed in italics, these words will frequently be explained in the text itself, but may often be found in the Glossary unit together with cross-references to related terms.

Suggested Background Texts in Cognition
Baddeley, A.D. (1976). *The Psychology of Memory*. New York: Basic Books.
Dodd, D.H., and White, R.M. (1980). *Cognition*. Boston: Allyn and Bacon.
Eysenck, M.W. (1984). *A Handbook of Cognitive Psychology*. London: Lawrence Erlbaum Associates.
Martindale, C. (1981). *Cognition and Consciousness*. Homewood, Illinois: Dorsey.
Neisser, U. (1967). *Cognitive Psychology*. New York: Appleton-Century-Crofts.
Neisser, U. (1976). *Cognition and Reality*. San Francisco: Freeman.
Seamon, J.G. (1980). *Memory and Cognition*. New York: Oxford.
Wingfield, A., and Byrnes, D.L. (1981). *The Psychology of Human Memory*. New York: Academic.

Suggested Background Texts in Statistics and Experimental Methodology
Anderson, D.C., and Borkowski, J.G. (1978). *Experimental Psychology*. Glenview, Illinois: Scott, Foresman.
Christensen, L.B. (1980). *Experimental Methodology*. Boston: Allyn and Bacon.
Cohen, L., and Holliday, M. (1982). *Statistics for Social Scientists*. London: Harper and Row.
Elmes, D.G., Kantowitz, B.H., Roediger, H.L. (1985). *Research Methods in Psychology*. St Paul: West.
Greene, J., and D'Oliveira, M. (1982). *Learning to use Statistical Tests in Psychology*. London: Harper and Row.
Kirk, R.(1968). *Experimental Design: Procedures for the Behavioral Sciences*. Belmont, Cal.: Brooks,Cole.
Winer, B.J. (1970). *Statistical Principles in Experimental Design*. London: McGraw Hill.

Computer Usage

"Why do we have to use computers? I thought this was a Psychology course."
The reason is quite simple. Psychology is about people. It is about how people work: how they process information and how they react to different situations. It concerns what happens when a person is confronted with a stimulus, whether that stimulus is a simple flash of light or the news that war has broken out. It involves finding out exactly what they do and exactly how they do it.

Exactness imposes costs however. It entails studying aspects of behaviour under closely controlled conditions so that valid conclusions may be drawn from any data gathered and any observations made. There is no point in carrying out an experiment unless the conclusions you draw from it have some basis in reality. The computer allows the presentation of stimuli to experimental subjects and the recording of the subjects' resulting responses in a controlled and consistent manner.

The computer also saves time, both the experimenter's time and the subject's time. Most of the experiments you will carry out involve procedures of randomization of stimulus sequences. You could carry out these experiments without the aid of a computer. You could use a tachistoscope rather than a computer screen for a lot of the experiments. You would, however, have to make up printed cards or photographic slides of each stimulus very carefully. You would have to sort these into a randomized presentation order. You would then have to present these, on the tachistoscope, to your subject and make a note of the response the subject made together with the reaction time which you would read off a timer. When the experiment was finished you would have to de-randomize all the subject's responses and then do a lot of boring and error-prone arithmetic in order to find out what had happened. As you may imagine these procedures take inordinate amounts of time. It is better that you spend your time gaining experience of different experiments, reading the literature and thinking of the implications of the results of the experiments than that you spend it in carrying out inconsequential chores.

The computer is there to serve you in your quest for knowledge of nature. It will do the dirty work, you can make the executive decisions and draw the brilliant conclusions. All you have to do is to learn how to use the beast. This is not difficult. You are not expected to become a computer wizard overnight nor at all. Using computers has nothing whatsoever to do with mathematics, arithmetic, programming, or the complex logical thought patterns of an order which you may deem yourself incapable of reaching. The skills that will be of most use to you in making use of computers for this course are the ability to follow instructions closely and the ability to type, even extremely slowly, with at least one finger. Other useful qualities are patience with and compassion for a dumb machine that is trying to do its best and the ability to recognize that you, yourself, may have made a dumb mistake.

It may be that you are familiar with the computer you are going to use for the course or perhaps you have never used a computer before. Whatever, there are a few things about computers that you should know. Makes and models of computers differ from one another in various ways but there are certain features that are generally common to almost all. Some of the important points are described below.

Health

A computer can be damaged by bashing it with a hammer, by spilling coffee on it, by jumping on it, by setting it alight, by throwing it out of the window to see if it bounces and by other such violent outbursts of behaviour. Indeed, when you use a computer, even though you have come to love the machine dearly, you may occasionally feel that you would be justified in cleaving it with an axe. You should not indulge in such actions, even though they may satisfy your blood lust and craving for revenge, as it can be expensive to repair or replace the machines and, deep down inside, you wouldn't really be happy being responsible for the death of a bright-eyed, innocent, little machine.

Sometimes a computer and its associated bits and pieces of hardware or software can be damaged by you tapping the wrong key at the wrong time or by you giving an erroneous command. If this is the case then the computer system you are using has not been designed well. Even though you typed the fatal command, you may consider yourself to be free of all blame or responsibility for the injury and console yourself with righteous indignation in your desolation.

A more common way for a computer to experience damage is by spontaneous degeneration. This is where the computer breaks down all by itself without any human intervention. Computers are masters of this art together with the art of disguise, where they can act exactly like perfectly healthy specimens when an engineer is about, only to

Computer Usage

be found writhing in pain and self-pity by the simple user who happens along next. Some experienced users have been known to have felt justified in wielding the above-mentioned axe to put the little beast out of its misery on such occasions, but don't you let the machine undermine your morale in this way. Persevere and it will probably get fed up with such silly games.

The most frequent ailment to assail computers is where they seem to go wrong but haven't really done so. What has happened here is that the user's assessment of the situation that the machine is not working is because the user either doesn't know what to do, doesn't know how to do it, is suffering from spontaneous degeneration due to an irrational fear of computers, is in love, or is suffering from the repercussions of yesterday evening. Luckily, however, if the system is well designed, no great damage will be done to the poor little computer by the insensitive user. At worst, the user will probably just waste her or his own time.

The purpose of the foregoing paragraphs is to attempt to absolve you in advance of all blame for any serious malfunctions which may occur in the computers you will be using in carrying out the experiments in this book. Violence excepted, any major malfunctions will not be your fault (they may not be anyone else's fault either). Minor malfunctions may be caused by you but are likely to inconvenience no-one but yourself. So please do not be afraid, as some people are, to approach a computer and tap its keys. You may type the wrong thing but it is extremely unlikely that you will do any harm.

The On/Off Switch
Oft repeated dialogue: *"The computer's not working."* *"Well switch it on then!"*

The Screen
This may be a separate unit from the computer itself and can often be switched on and off independently. It will normally have contrast and brightness controls which should not be set too high. Items on the screen should be clearly visible and the background should be dark and certainly not glowing. If in doubt, turn the contrast and/or brightness down. If you are getting no picture and the computer is switched on, then check that the screen is switched on too. Next try the contrast and brightness controls. You should not work in a darkened room. Try to attain a level of ambient illumination whereby you can read this book easily, but is not sufficiently bright to cause difficulty in reading text on the screen. Don't feel that you have to adjust the controls every time you use the computer, as in most cases they will be correctly set.

During the course of these experiments you will often be asked to keep your head at a certain distance from the screen. This is not requested in order to make you feel uncomfortable but in order that the visual stimuli fall on certain areas of your retina. It is sometimes difficult to maintain a particular head-screen distance without the aid of a chin rest or other support, but try to do the best you can. If you don't roughly maintain the distances suggested in the experimental instructions then some of the experiments are likely to produce personal results which are at variance with the summary of group results quoted to you by the computer. Use a ruler where possible and perhaps a length of string when the distance is greater than 30 cm (12").

The Keyboard
The keyboard is your means of communicating your instructions to the computer so be sure to know how to use it. You don't have to be a great typist to use the keyboard and, if you are, you may have to unlearn a few things.

There are certain keys and combinations of keys whose functions are not immediately apparent and there are certain ways of using the keys that you will find useful. A combination of keys involves holding down two or more keys more or less simultaneously. That is, one of the keys is held down and the other is then tapped and then both are released. In the following descriptions the legend on the key is shown in capitals and combinations are connected by a dash, with the key which has to be pressed first and held down whilst the other key is tapped, appearing before the dash. If there does not seem to be a key, with the legend referred to on your computer, then you will have to consult an instructor or the computer's manual to find out which key is relevant. The first set of combinations involves the use of the SHIFT key. Some keys show more than one character on their surface. A SHIFTed combination usually produces the character shown at the top of the key surface. Thus SHIFT-5 may produce % and SHIFT-/ may produce ?. The actual combinations on your computer may be different. Often you get a lower-case letter by typing an alphabetic key and an upper-case (capital) letter by pressing SHIFT-(alphabetic key). On the other hand, some keyboards will only produce upper-case letters. Another set of combinations involves the CTRL (sometimes CONTROL or similar) key. CTRL-G often rings or beeps the computer's bell. CTRL combinations are usually varied in their effects from computer to computer and indeed from time to time, but don't worry about this – it is enough to know that you may be expected to remember at most a few CTRL combinations for your computer.

Of the computer keys which have special functions, either by themselves or in combination with others the RETURN key is the most important. Sometimes this key bears the legend ENTER rather than return and sometimes it is simply identified by this shape :

The return key is used to tell the computer that the command you were typing is now complete and that it may begin processing it. Say, for example, the computer asked you how many cars there were parked in the street outside. Let us say there were 10 of them. You begin to respond by pressing the "1" key. Now you don't want the computer to jump in and say "Aha! there's one car out there. Thank you very much and goodbye." You have still to press the "0" key, but how does the computer know this, and, once you have pressed it, how does it know that you are now finished and don't wish to press another key – there may be 109 cars outside. The convention that humans and computers have generally agreed on, is that when a human is typing in a command to a computer or is responding to a request for information, then the computer will not attempt to act on the command till the RETURN key has been pressed. This also allows the human to correct typing mistakes before the command or response is processed.

Find out how to fix minor typing errors on your machine. The correction of typing errors normally involves the use of one or more other special keys. DELete is a key often used to delete the last character you typed, and sometimes a backspace key is used to back you up to the character, which you can then delete and replace by another character merely by typing the new character over the old one. Sometimes the DELete key is identified by this symbol:

There may be various other keys with special functions. These functions can often change according to the context in which they are used. Though normally working much like a typewriter, in fact all the keys on the keyboard can have their functions changed to suit what is currently happening. This is often the case in our experiments. The Y key may be designated to mean "Yes" and the N key to mean "No" in some experiments and pressing any other key may have no effect till the experiment is finished. Often during experiments the computer knows that a response by a human will involve only one key press and therefore it does not wait for the RETURN key to be pressed.

There is often a RESET key on the keyboard. If you find yourself in the middle of some thing that you shouldn't be in the middle of and you want to get back to the beginning or to some recognizable state of affairs, then pressing the RESET or equivalent key will probably get you there. Find out how to recover control of the computer once you have lost it. If all else fails, of course, you can always switch off and on again, but that's a bit like giving in.

Common mistakes: The computer has separate keys for the numeral 0 and for the letter O. Do not confuse these. It also has separate keys for the letter l, the letter I, and the number 1. Don't confuse these either. Don't hold a key down for extended periods, always tap it crisply. Various computers will act in different ways to a key which is depressed for a longish time.

Finally, don't be too hard on the keyboard. In the experiments you will often be asked to respond as quickly as you can to some stimulus by pressing a key on the keyboard. This means exactly what it says. It does not mean that you should respond with maximum force and thump the keys, as this is likely to damage the keyboard and will certainly slow you down, involving, as it does, the control of larger muscle groups in the body.

Computer Usage

Summary of Computer Use

The administrative details of how, when and where you can use the computer are outside the scope of this book. As the software runs on a number of different makes and models of computer, stand-alone computers and networked ones, precise details of exactly how you get the programs to start cannot be given here. Your tutor or system administrator will, no doubt, enlighten you on the above points.

When the package starts running the screen will show a title and copyright notice and will ask you to type a key. There may be other notices following this, each one ending by asking you to type a key. Finally the screen will show a MENU such as the one below:

```
              MENU

    0  :   *** STOP ***
    2  :   WORD FREQUENCY
    3  :   WATERFALL EFFECT
       :
       :   etc.
       :
       :   SUBLIMINAL PERCEPTION
       :   *** TEST QUESTIONS ***
```

Type the number of your choice then press the <RETURN> key

You answer the question by typing in the number of the option you require (followed by RETURN). Answering 0 will stop this suite of programs and return the computer to the Operating System. In the example above, answering with a number between 1 and 11 will start the program which runs the experiment for the particular unit you are doing. Answering 12 will bring up another menu which pertains to the multiple choice questions.

Assuming you pick a number between 1 and 11 the relevant experiment will begin, preceded by instructions and perhaps practice trials. After the experiment is complete you will normally be given a summary of your results together with the results of some subjects who preceded you in doing the experiment. These data should be copied into the relevant tables in this book. You will then be returned once more to the Menu.

Had you picked option 12 from the above menu, a different menu would have been displayed which would have allowed you to pick a set of multiple choice questions to answer. There is one set of questions for each experimental unit. The "zero" option on this menu returns to the previous menu, also known as the "main menu".

You should only attempt to answer the multiple choice questions when you have completed the experimental work of the unit, carried out any statistical analysis which is required and consulted some of the references to gain background information. As distributed the multiple choice options have 10 questions per unit. Each question presents 4 alternative answers. You are expected to pick one answer from those presented as your choice of the correct or best answer. Your course tutor, however, may have altered the number of questions per unit to suit the course taught at your institution.

Being a Subject

As was stated earlier, exactness has its costs. One of the costs to you will be that you, or perhaps a friend, will have to act as subject in the various experiments. This can often be interesting and is valuable experience. It's fine reading about experiments in text books or journals but it is often enlightening to experience what subjects have to go through. Being a subject in some experiments can be exhausting and occasionally rather tedious. This is one of the costs of gathering sufficient data for statistical analysis.

You should be aware that people in general find it very difficult to follow experimental instructions when acting as subject. Read the instructions carefully or make sure your subject has read them carefully before starting the task proper. This advice cannot be overstressed.

You or your subject can, of course, easily make a purposeful mess of an experiment (the "screw-you" effect). That, of course, requires no skill or ability at all. Part of what you should try to learn whilst doing these experiments is how to play the being-a-subject game and how to instruct other people in the art of being-a-subject.

Getting Through the Experiments

The experiments should be followed in order. The administrative details of how, when and where you can use the computer are without the remit of this book, but you should realize that some experiments will take half an hour or so to run. Plan your time on the computer accordingly. You don't want to have to leave when you have completed three-quarters of an experiment. This is especially true if you have managed to persuade someone else to come along to act as subject for you.

Try to answer the questions in each chapter and do what statistical analysis is required as soon as you can after completing the experiment or after you have debriefed your subject, i.e. when your memory of the events are fresh.

Experimental Report Writing

The production and understanding of experimental reports is a fundamental part of the working psychologist's life. This is because psychology attempts to adopt the experimental method of scientific investigation wherever possible and the outcomes of such investigations are normally communicated in scientific reports. The most common type of report is that describing one or more scientific experiments and such reports are published in journals such as Cognitive Psychology. Other types of communication document include the reports of a clinical or educational psychologist about their clients and reports by government committees. This chapter will concentrate on how to write reports that are in the style of journal articles since publishing articles is such an essential part of the psychologist's role. Writing in this style will have the additional advantage of providing some carry over to other kinds of writing, since practice will be obtained in presenting facts and ideas in a logical, coherent manner and in developing an economical writing style.

The purpose of the journal article is largely to permit dissemination of both the experimental results and the theoretical ideas of a particular experimenter, so that the scientific community at large can benefit from the knowledge and ideas the article contains, thus permitting further related thinking and experimenting. However, it also provides the experimenter with a formal statement of his own work and is therefore invaluable even where publication is not intended.

The essence of an experimental report is that it provides a detailed record of what the experimenter did, why he did it, what he found and what he concluded from this. A standard format has evolved to get this essential information across as simply and effectively as possible and most articles can be seen to conform fairly closely to this standard. This allows the writer a familiar layout within which he can set out his material and helps ensure that essential information is not overlooked, while permitting the reader to find the information he requires with the minimum of effort.

The appropriate style or format involves dividing the report into sections, each of which has a specific function:

Title
Abstract
Introduction
Method
   Design
   Subjects
   Apparatus
   Stimuli
   Procedure
Results
Discussion
References
Appendices

We shall look at each of these sections in turn and you can turn to the sample report, which is included as the next chapter, for the application of many of the principles discussed. More detailed information is available from the large number of textbooks on Experimental Design and Methodology that have been published. Some specific recommendations are included in the Reference section at the end of this chapter.

Title

The title represents the first page of a report that is being submitted for publication or the first few lines at the top of a published one. In the former case the title page is not numbered. The title selected should be as brief and informative as possible, helping the reader to know what the contents of the report are. This can frequently be achieved by stating the independent and dependent variables as well as the relationship between them. The subjects being tested should also receive a mention, particularly if they are not adult humans. If they are it is usual to assume this unless the subjects constitute a very unusual sample.

Some examples of informative titles are:
> **Attention in the human infant: effects of complexity and perimeter.**
> **Encoding differences in recall and recognition.**
> **Killing elicited by brain stimulation in rats.**

Uninformative titles may take these forms:
> **This study is an experimental investigation of memory.**
> **Cat personality.**

In a report being submitted for publication, the title will be followed by the name/s of the researcher/s together with their affiliation, i.e. the name of the institution within which they work and usually its address. In a published report, this information is usually included in a footnote together with any suitable acknowledgements, for example, to a scientific body who provided funds for the work being reported.

Abstract

The abstract or summary is the last thing the experimenter writes, but it should appear at the beginning of the article itself so that an interested reader can quickly determine whether the contents are likely to be of use to him. Indeed in the present scientific situation of escalating publication volume there is no way that the researcher can read every article in full that may be of some interest. Therefore, the abstract allows at least the main aspects of the study to be understood, even if much of the fine detail is not obtained. In addition, it usually helps to have read a brief overview before trying to understand the main text.

The abstract should be no longer than 175 words, but will usually be shorter. It should cover all the essential information contained in the report and thus will provide a summary of each of the principle sections. The main components of the abstract will therefore be a short statement of the problem being investigated, the design used, the subjects investigated, the stimulus materials involved and any important apparatus, the principal results obtained and their analysis together with the main conclusions drawn.

This perhaps sounds like a tall-order, but with practice it will become fairly straightforward. Have a look at a number of published articles to see how abstracts are typically written and what relationship they bear to the articles themselves.

Introduction

The introduction is rarely labelled and in an unpublished report simply starts on a new page after the title page. Its purpose is to provide the background to the experiment, starting at a fairly general level and focusing down to the very specific detail that is needed to introduce the experiment to be described. The background material will usually be drawn from journal articles and books and will be restricted to the most relevant selection. There is no need to review every article in the area, that is the function of a literature review article or perhaps a PhD thesis. Nor is it sensible to give all the details of the few reports selected, only those details which help to introduce your experiment are required. An attempt should usually be made to produce a critical appraisal of the research sampled.

It cannot be too strongly emphasized that the material you introduce must lead in a direct way into your experiment, letting the reader know what the area is about, why it is worth looking at and why your particular experiment is an interesting or valuable one to undertake. The introduction should therefore end up with a clear statement of the question/s under investigation. One of the best ways to do this is to formally state the *null hypothesis*, or perhaps better in terms of clarity, the *experimental hypothesis*.

Do not under any circumstances include any material about the conduct or the results of the experiment to be described. This information must be kept for the Methods and Results section.

Methods

The Methods section contains all the information required by another investigator to replicate the experiment being described and therefore gives a detailed account of the practical aspects of conducting the experiment under a set of subheadings. The subheadings that we will look at are the most common, but certainly do not fit all experimental reports and can therefore be altered as necessary. The normal subheadings are:

Design

This section may sometimes be placed towards the end of the Methods section and be combined with the Procedure, although it may usefully be kept separate. In most published papers the Design section is very brief. When more detail is required, it should cover the conditions studied in the experiment, the independent variable/s, and the dependent variable/s. Was each subject tested under one/some/all conditions and how were subjects actually allocated to each condition (e.g. randomly or through counterbalancing)?

Subjects

This section gives information about what type of subjects were tested (e.g. adult hooded rats; social class IV male adults), how they were selected from the population, how many there were, what ages (*mean* and *range*), and what sex they were. Other subject details may be required in particular studies. In many cases it will also be necessary to provide details of those subjects who failed to complete the experiment and for what reasons.

Apparatus

The idea of this section is to allow other researchers to purchase or construct equivalent apparatus. Give details of all the *important* equipment that was used, naming the psychometric tests or the commercial equipment used and giving its supplier (e.g. Electronics Developments Corporation 3-field tachistoscope, model number 281) and describing as fully as required any custom-built equipment. Do not mention items like paper and pencils unless they are an essential part of the apparatus. An illustrative diagram with appropriate dimensions may often be helpful. What type of measure did the equipment provide (reaction time in *msec*)?

Stimuli

This section may sometimes be incorporated within the apparatus section but the information may be clearer in a separate section. Any specially prepared stimulus materials should be described in all relevant aspects, with information about how the materials were selected and constructed. A photograph or illustrative diagram will often be very valuable.

Procedure

The procedure explains what happened from the point of contacting the subjects to their leaving the experimental situation. This information on the order of events should allow another experimenter to exactly replicate the sequence of your experiment, covering the actions of both experimenter and subjects. Any instructions to subjects should be briefly summarized and a full statement included as an appendix with a suitable reference to the appendix in the text (e.g. Full instructions are included in Appendix 2.).

Results

The Results section provides a summary of the data obtained (remember that datum is single and data is plural). It also describes the analytic procedures that were used to test the data for reliability. It is difficult to describe a simple formula for creating a good results section, since the best form will usually vary from experiment to experiment. However, the following may serve as a guide:

1. Start by repeating the experimental hypothesis/es in order to direct attention to the relevant aspects of the data. This is rarely done in published reports, however.

2. Provide a summary of the data (e.g. means, medians, correlations) that are relevant to the hypothesis/es just stated. These are *descriptive* statistics. Never present raw data in the results section, but place it in an appendix if you think it is required and refer to it in the results section. Presentation of the summary data

may be best achieved by using text combined with either graphs or tables of data. These should make sense without reference to the text itself and must always have an explanatory title above or below, for example:

Table 1. *Mean reaction times for four groups of subjects from a simple reaction time task.*

3. Where *inferential* statistics have been applied, i.e. tests of reliability have been carried out to test specific hypotheses or simply to "trawl" for interesting results, you need to provide information about the outcome, give the name of the test used (e.g. a matched-pairs t-test), and the relevant derived statistic, (e.g. the t-value). *Degrees of freedom* and the associated *probability value* will also be required and these are usually written in the following manner:

". . . a significant t-value was obtained (t = 3.89, $d.f.$ = 20, $p < 0.001$, two-tailed test) in the comparison between the mean values of the subjects in group A and group B . . .".

You will note that the statistic t is highlighted by being printed in italics as is the probability p. It is common practice to italicize, underline or otherwise highlight such statistics. In your case, underlining would be the most appropriate method.

4. Make a brief statement of the implications of the obtained results for the hypotheses being considered, but do not try to interpret or discuss these results at this stage.

Discussion

This should commence with a concise summary of the results obtained and be followed by an interpretation of these results in terms of the experimental hypotheses. The discussion should relate these conclusions to any theoretical model mentioned in the introduction on which the experiment was based and to any competing models or theories. Following this, discuss anything that still requires explanation especially if the hypotheses were not upheld in the experiment.

Cover any possible weaknesses in the experiment mentioned, for example, are there any sources of uncontrolled error whose effects may be important? Mention only the most important factors and do it in a constructive manner.

What implications does your work have for further research. Suggest other experiments that could be carried out to follow up any important discoveries from the experiment described. Are there any potential practical applications of the research, could it be developed in any particularly interesting ways?

It is *very important* that you realise that experimental results that are not significant and do not therefore support the experimental hypotheses are nevertheless valuable. It is very useful to know that a particular hypothesis cannot be easily supported, particularly if the study is a replication of a previously supportive study. This may indicate undisclosed methodological problems or it may suggest that the phenomenon under investigation is not a robust one or was mistakenly supported in the previous study.

End your discussion with a brief summary statement of the main conclusions arrived at on the basis of the experimental results.

References

All papers or books mentioned in the text must be reported in full in the reference section, and not in footnotes.

A. When mentioned in the text, references are usually found in one of the following forms:

(i) Jason (1981) stated that . . .

(ii) Recently, several studies have supported this connection between A and B (Abrahamson, 1963; Jason, 1981; Zallop & Duncan, 1978). *(Note the use of alphabetic order and not date order in multiple references).*

(iii) In two studies, Jason (1981a; 1981b) reported . . . *(Here there are two papers from the same author in the same year).*

B. If a quotation from the original text is made, then the page from which the quotation is drawn must also be stated:

Jason (1981) believes that " . . . man is quite obviously fundamentally different from woman in a number of important psychological respects." (p. 256).

C. All the references previously cited must be credited in the reference section in alphabetical order, with the titles of books and journals emphasized by either being printed in *italics*, or underlined. In addition the volume number of a journal is usually emphasized in a similar manner. Some examples of books and articles that are relevant to experimental design, statistical analysis and report writing are as follows:

Anderson, D.C., and Borkowski, J.G. (1978). *Experimental Psychology.* Glenview: Scott, Foresman.
Barber, T.X., and Silver, M.J. (1968). Fact, fiction and the experimenter bias effect. *Psychological Bulletin Monograph, 70,* 1-29.
Christensen, L.B. (1980). *Experimental Methodology.* Boston: Allyn & Bacon.
Fallik, F., and Brown, B. (1983). *Statistics for Behavioral Sciences.* Homewood, Illinois: Dorsey.
Greene, J., and D'Olivera, M. (1982). *Learning to use Statistical Tests in Psychology.* London: Harper & Row.

Appendices

These are started on new pages and are headed with the appropriate number and a descriptive title which indicates the contents. For example:

Appendix 1. Raw data from an experiment into simple reaction time.

Report Presentation

When you are writing a report, follow the recommendations given above and try to present it in the best possible manner. The reports to be entered in this book cannot obviously be typed, but in other circumstances, the report should always be typed, double-spaced on one side of the paper only, with a 2 inch margin all round. If you are using graphs, make them as professional as possible since this can make a large difference to a presentation. Number each page of the report, starting after the title page and staple all the pages together or secure them in some kind of binding.

Reference

American Psychological Association. (1983). *Publication Manual of the American Psychological Association (3rd Edition).* Washington D.C.: Author.

# Sample Report

This chapter consists of a short and fairly straightforward article prepared in a form that would be suitable for submission to many psychological journals to be considered for publication. It is not meant to be a perfect model for all write-ups, but should provide examples to illustrate some of the points raised in the previous chapter. You would be well advised to look closely at a number of recent journals to see how much written reports have in common and how much variation there is. Look also at the page in each journal which provides guidance about that particular journal's recommended report format. It will usually be headed "Instructions to Authors" and will be found normally at the beginning or at the end of the journal.

The perception of wholes and parts by the human neonate.

Bushnell, I.W.R.[1], Slater, A.[2], Morison, V.[2], and Rose, D.[2]

[1] Department of Psychology
University of Glasgow

[2] Department of Psychology
University of Exeter

Reprint requests should be sent to Dr.I.W.R. Bushnell, Department of Psychology, University of Glasgow, Glasgow G12 8QT, United Kingdom. Senior authorship is shared between the first two authors with precedence of names being decided on the toss of a coin. We would like to thank the Social Science Research Council for support of the Exeter portion of this work under grant number C00232114. Our grateful appreciation is also extended to the staff of the respective Maternity Hospitals for their invaluable cooperation and to Margaret Brawley and Joanne Stockbridge for their assistance with testing.

Abstract

While it is known that newborn babies can discriminate between simple shapes, an important question concerning innate and early perception is whether such discriminations are made on the basis of processing of the whole shape or of its component parts. Two experiments are described in which part/whole perception was investigated with newborn subjects. In both experiments the stimuli were large triangles or crosses made up either from small triangles or small crosses and an infant-controlled habituation procedure was used. The results demonstrated that newborns can detect, and respond to changes in, both the whole and the parts of the stimuli used. It is suggested that newborns inherit a structured foundation which acts to organize perception from birth.

The majority of research with young infants has emphasized their limitations. The newborn baby is claimed to process little more than high-contrast edges and his attention is "captured" by salient and rather simple characteristics of stimulation. Underlying this approach is the assumption that the infant has to construct an organized world out of the welter of impinging information received by the sensory systems.

One important aspect of perceptual organization that is therefore denied the young infant is pattern perception or configuration processing. Salapatek (1975), for example, draws this conclusion from experimental data suggesting that young infants tend to direct their scanning towards a single feature of a stimulus such as a triangle and make few eye movements around the preferred fixation point (Salapatek & Kessen, 1966). In addition he points out that the fixations of infants under 2 months-of-age appear to be dominated by contour density and numerosity. This leads him to adopt the position that infants less than 1 to 2 months-of-age only respond to and process preferred elements in the visual array rather than whole figures. Of course this does appear to presuppose the adoption of a motor-copy model of perception requiring that active scanning takes place to provide information about the contours making up a figure. It remains possible that infants need only look with a minimum of eye movements to obtain certain kinds of form information. This certainly holds true for older children and for adults (Luria & Strauss, 1978). Naturally it could still be argued that the ability to perceive whole forms without active scanning is a learned ability which depends upon a great deal of experience and therefore develops very slowly.

What evidence then does exist concerning the development of the ability to respond to the "arrangement or pattern of figural elements"? There have been a number of studies which have looked at infants' response to pattern information such as curvature. These studies typically report a preference for curvilinear pattern over rectilinear from the 8th week of life (Fantz, 1958; Fantz & Miranda, 1975; Ruff & Turkewitz, 1975). This may be mediated directly by the activation of feature receptors specific to curvature (Hubel & Weisel, 1965; Pribram, 1973; Riggs, 1974) although a study by Fantz & Nevis (1967) found a preference for a concentric, circular arrangement of straight line segments over a number of other arrangements.

There are also many studies which have used schematic faces as stimuli with the intention of demonstrating a special response to the face configuration. One study of particular note is that of Goren, Sarty & Wu (1975) in which infants of only minutes-of-age demonstrated a preference for a facelike organization of features over moderately scrambled and severely scrambled organizations. However, there has been at least one failure to replicate this study (Bushnell, Chisholm & O'Donnell, 1981) and conflicting results have been reported from studies with older infants (Fantz, 1965, 1966; Haaf, 1974; Haaf & Brown, 1976; Hershenson, 1965; Jones-Molfese, 1975; McCall & Kagan, 1967; Maurer & Barrera, 1981). Certainly this conflict in results makes it hard to draw conclusions about pattern perception and in any event it may be that the response to facelike stimuli is a special case. The research on neonatal imitation of facial gestures (Meltzoff & Moore, 1977) appears to reinforce this view and supports the speculation that infants may inherit some kind of "template" of the human face: if Goren et al.'s preference results can be substantiated they suggest just this kind of conclusion.

If other kinds of stimuli are considered there is some support for a reasonably early response to pattern arrangement. While Bower (1966) found no response to the configuration of a geometric stimulus until 16 weeks-of-age, Maisel & Karmel (1978) reported that infants from at least 5-6 weeks could discriminate between geometric stimuli on the basis of configurational differences although this could be easily confounded by contour density disparity. Slater, Morison & Rose (1983) have shown that neonates discriminate amongst a set of geometric shapes and this implies that some level of pattern perception is present at birth, but whether this is based on part or whole perception is not clear. The following experiments were therefore intended to consider more closely the development of the configurational response by looking at newborn infants' processing of geometric shapes. Stimuli were used in which the elements or parts could be the same as, or different from, the shape of the whole stimulus. This was intended to allow specification of whether or not the newborn is able to detect wholes or parts of stimuli and to provide a test of Salapatek's (1975) statement that "...the very early perception of two-dimensional visual stimuli must be regarded as the perception of parts rather than wholes." (p. 226).

EXPERIMENT 1

This study was designed to investigate whether neonates are capable of discriminating between two stimuli whose overall shapes are the same but whose parts are different. If the position taken by Salapatek (1975) is correct, neonates should focus on the figural elements and if any differences can be detected it should be evident at this level. An infant control habituation paradigm was adopted for assessing discrimination (Horowitz, Paden, Bhana & Self, 1972).

Sample Report

Subjects

Infants were volunteered by their mothers at the Royal Maternity Hospital, Glasgow and the Exeter Royal Hospital. None of the infants tested had any medical problems and all were alert and responsive at the time of testing. Testing was equally divided between Glasgow and Exeter so that 12 infants (7 male and 5 female) were tested at each location. The average age of the subjects was 3 days 8 hours (range 19 to 339 hours). A further 21 subjects were selected, but failed to complete the test procedure due to state problems.

Stimuli

The four achromatic stimuli are shown in Fig. 1 and constitute:

1. A large cross made up from nine small crosses
2. A large triangle made up from nine small crosses
3. A large cross made up from nine small triangles
4. A large triangle made up from nine small triangles.

Fig. 1. *Representation of the stimuli adopted in Experiment 1. (The stimulus figures are not to scale).*

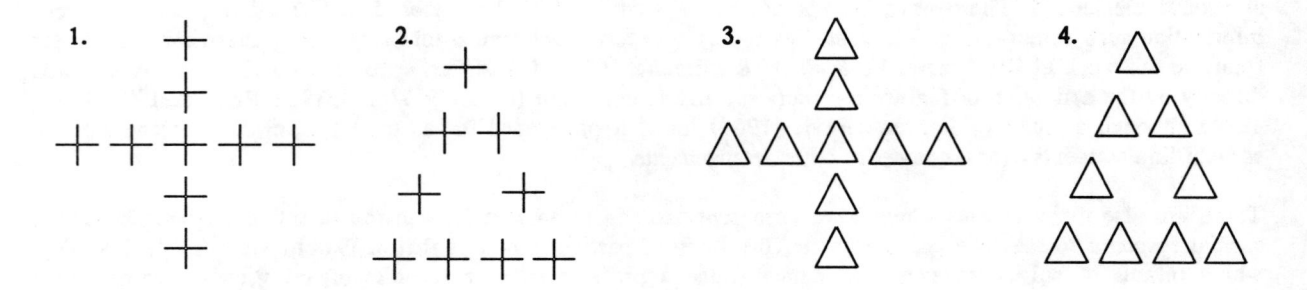

The overall width and height of each stimulus figure was 12.8 cm with each element measuring 2.2 cm. At a viewing distance of 30 cm the whole figure subtended 23 degrees and each part subtended 4.2 degrees. Under the conditions of testing the luminances of the white stimulus background and the dark contour were respectively, 36 and 6 foot-lamberts.

Apparatus/Procedure

An infant control procedure was used where the infant determined the course of the habituation trials. Each infant was brought to a quiet experimental room in the maternity ward of the respective hospital and positioned on one experimenter's knee, with the infant's eyes 30 cm from the stimulus screen. When the baby was settled, one of the four stimuli, previously selected according to a counterbalanced design as the habituation stimulus, was presented by a second experimenter and the first trial began when the baby was judged to have looked at the stimulus. The trial ended only when the infant looked away for a period of 2 sec. or more. The next trial began with the next fixation and this sequence continued until the baby was judged to have habituated. This was held to have occurred when the duration of looking on any three successive trials (from the fourth trial on) totalled 50% or less than the total of the first three. Following criterion the babies were given paired presentations for two trials of both the old and a new stimulus where the parts were changed. Each trial lasted until 20 sec. of looking had accumulated. The stimuli were shown in both right and left positions, the positions being reversed from trial 1 to trial 2, and counterbalanced across subjects. There were four conditions in all, with equal numbers of subjects tested in each. The habituation stimulus and, in parentheses, the stimulus pair presented on the post-criterion trials and numbered as in Fig. 1, were:

1(1, 3); 2 (2, 4); 3 (3, 1); 4 (4, 2).

During these post-criterion trials the experimenter holding the baby looked away from the stimulus screen so that knowledge about which stimulus the baby fixated was not available. A previous study (Slater, Morison and Rose, 1983) has shown excellent inter-observer agreement when recording infant's fixation using this procedure (Pearson's r=0.87, p<0.001).

Results

The data for the two post-criterion test periods were combined to provide a total fixation time to the familiar stimulus and to the novel stimulus (see Table 1). Overall, 62% of the time was spent viewing the novel stimulus, a preference for novelty that was significant using a correlated t-test (t=2.35, $d.f.$=23, p<0.025, one-tailed test).

Table 1. *Mean fixation times (sec.) to novel and familiar stimuli.*

	Stimulus	
	Familiar	Novel
	15.54	24.46
	SD = 9.28	

Discussion

The significant novelty preference means that the change to the parts of the stimuli was detected. This is in accord with the suggestion of Salapatek (1975) that early perception is focused on the elements constituting an overall pattern.

EXPERIMENT 2

The next aspect tested was the infant's ability to detect the overall pattern in the present stimuli and to respond to a change in the whole while the parts remained the same. An habituation paradigm was again adopted.

Subjects

Infants were obtained from the same sources, with testing equally divided between Glasgow and Exeter. There were 12 infants tested (4 male and 8 female) with an average age of 4 days 2 hours (range 25-185 hours). A further 8 infants failed to complete testing due to problems of state or due to side bias in their data.

Stimuli

The original stimuli were retained with the novel stimulus now involving a change in the whole shape rather than the parts. Thus if a subject was familiarized to stimulus 1, he would receive stimulus 2 as the novel stimulus and vice versa; subjects familiarized to stimulus 3 received stimulus 4 as the novel stimulus and vice versa. Full counterbalancing of stimuli was maintained.

Results

The data for the two post-criterion test periods were combined (see Table 2) and analysed using a correlated t-test. Overall, 67.4% of the time was spent viewing the novel shape, a preference that was significant (t=4.1, $d.f.$=11, p<0.005, one-tailed test).

Table 2. Mean fixation times (sec.) to novel and familiar stimuli.

$$\begin{array}{cc} \multicolumn{2}{c}{\text{Stimulus}} \\ \text{Familiar} & \text{Novel} \\ 13.04 & 26.96 \end{array}$$

$$SD = 5.88$$

Discussion

The results of Experiments 1 and 2 present quite clear evidence that neonates were able to respond not only at the level of parts, but also to the overall configuration of those parts. This is an ability which has been previously denied the young infant. It could be assumed from this information that newborn infants do not have to totally construct an organized visual world from an undifferentiated stream of low-level feature information. Rather it is suggested that infants are born with a visual system that encompasses a set of "in-built" processes which act to organize visual perception. For example, one such process might assist in determining figure-ground relations. Thus the infant could be said to inherit a structured foundation which acts to canalize further developments in which differentiation and classification processes undoubtedly play a major part.

The major task of researchers in this area is therefore to obtain further detailed information about the processes and capacities with which the neonate commences life in order that the developmental process can be examined in a meaningful way. As Hazlitt has commented "... the man who has heard the beginning of a story is ipso facto a more reliable judge of the credibility of the ending than the man who has come in at the middle" (quoted in Munn, 1955, p.VI).

References

Bower, T.G.R. (1966). Heterogeneous summation in human infants. *Animal Behavior, 14*, 395-398.

Bushnell, I.W.R., Chisholm, B., and O'Donnell, P. (1981). *Visual following and pattern configuration in neonates.* Unpublished research paper, University of Glasgow.

Fantz, R.L. (1958). Pattern vision in young infants. *Psychological Record, 8*, 43-49.

Fantz, R.L. Visual perception from birth as shown by pattern selectivity. *Annals of the New York Academy of Sciences*, 1965, *118*, 793-814.

Fantz, R.L. (1966). Pattern discrimination and selective attention as determinants of perceptual development from birth. In A.H. Kidd and J.L. Rivoire (Eds.), *Perceptual Development in Children*. New York:International.

Fantz, R.L., and Miranda, S.B. (1975). Newborn infant attention to form of contour. *Child Development, 46*, 224-228.

Fantz, R.L., and Nevis, S. (1967). Pattern preferences and perceptual-cognitive development in early infancy. *Merrill-Palmer Quarterly, 3*, 77-108.

Goren, C.C., Sarty, M., and Wu, P.Y.K. (1975). Visual following and pattern discrimination of face-like stimuli by newborn infants. *Pediatrics, 56*, 544-549.

Haaf, R.A. (1974). Complexity and facial resemblance as determinants of response to face-like stimuli by 5 and 10 week old infants. *Journal of Experimental Child Psychology, 18*, 480-487.

Haaf, R.A., and Brown, C.J. (1976). Infants' response to face-like patterns: Developmental changes between 10 and 15 weeks of age. *Journal of Experimental Child Psychology, 22*, 155-160.

Hershenson, M. (1965). Visual discrimination in the human newborn. *Dissertation Abstracts, 26*.

Horowitz, F.D., Paden, L., Bhana, K., and Self, P. (1972). An infant-control procedure for studying infant visual fixations. *Developmental Psychology, 7*, 90.

Hubel,D.H., and Weisel, T.N. (1965). Receptive fields and functional architecture in two nonstriate areas (18 and 19) of the cat. *Journal of Neurophysiology, 28*, 229-289.

Jones-Molfese, V. (1975). Preferences of infants for regular and distorted facial stimuli. *Child Development, 46*, 1005-1009.

Luria, S.M., and Strauss, M.S. (1978). Comparison of eye movements over faces in photographic positives and negatives. *Perception, 7*, 349-358.

McCall, R.B., and Kagan, J. (1967). Attention in the infant: effects of complexity, contour, perimeter and familiarity. *Child Development, 38,* 939-952.

Maisel, E.B., and Karmel, B.Z. (1978). Contour density and pattern configuration in visual preferences of infants. *Infant Behavior and Development, 1,* 127-140.

Maurer, D., and Barrera, M. (1981). Infants' perception of natural and distorted arrangements of a schematic face. *Child Development, 52,* 196-202.

Meltzoff, A.N., and Moore, M.K. (1977). Imitation of facial and manual gestures by human neonates. *Science, 198,* 75-78.

Munn, N. (1955). *The Evolution and Growth of Human Behavior.* Boston: Houghton Mifflin.

Pribram, K. H. (1973). The case for a brain electrodiagnostic in functional disorders. In S. Bogoch (Ed.), *Biological Diagnosis of Brain Disorders.* New York: Spectrum Halstead.

Riggs, L.A. (1974). Curvature detectors in human vision. *Science, 184,* 1200-1201.

Ruff, H.A., and Turkewitz, G. (1975). Developmental changes in the effectiveness of stimulus intensity on infant visual attention. *Developmental Psychology, 11,* 705-710.

Salapatek, P. (1975). Pattern perception in early infancy. In L.B. Cohen and P. Salapatek (Eds.), *Infant Perception from Sensation to Cognition.* New York: Academic, 1975.

Salapatek, P., and Kessen, W. (1966). Visual scanning of triangles by the human newborn. *Journal of Experimental Child Psychology, 3,* 155-167.

Slater, A., Morison, V., and Rose, D. (1983). Perception of shape by the new-born baby. *British Journal of Developmental Psychology, 1,* 135-142.

Chapter 1: Simple Reaction Time

A great number of both past and present experimental techniques used in Psychology depend on the accurate measurement of subjects' reaction time (the latency to respond to a rapidly presented stimulus) as the *dependent variable*. Usually the psychologist is not really interested in how quick someone is to press a button, but is interested in using reaction time as a measure of the time it takes to perform a mental operation. This has been termed *mental chronometry* (Posner & Rogers, 1978) and makes the assumption that the processing of information takes a certain amount of time and that if we increase the information processing load involved in a task then the response latency of subjects doing the task should be extended. Hence we can make testable predictions regarding the latencies of subjects doing particular tasks and use these data to test theories of mental behaviour.

Naturally there is a part of the response latency which is attributable to the efficiency of the subject's motor system (if you like, how quick he is with his hands), but we can arrange our experiment so that this factor will remain relatively constant across the *experimental conditions* while the mental processing component will vary.

A more important variable than *inter-individual variation*, however, is *intra-individual variation* where the individual subject's performance varies widely across time. This has the effect of introducing "noise" into the data thus making it harder when using a w*ithin subjects* design to obtain clear results to test a hypothesis. This is because it is not easy to tell if any differences between your conditions are due to chance intra-subject variations or to some real differences in the effect of the i*ndependent variables*. Fortunately there a number of sensitive statistical tests which have been designed for just this purpose - to tease out the influence of individual subject variance and variance attributable to experimental manipulation of the independent variables.

The present experiment is designed to introduce you to the reaction time paradigm and to demonstrate your own response variability (and that of a large group of other subjects) in the simplest of all experimental situations - *simple reaction time*, where the subject's only responsibility is to press a single button when an event occurs and little mental activity would seem to be involved.

To recap then, in the situation where the subject has to press a button in response to a visual stimulus such as a light appearing, there will be three major components to his reaction time:

1. The time it takes for the light stimulus to activate the photoreceptors in the retina and for the consequent nerve impulse to reach the processing areas within the brain.

2. The time that is required for central processes to occur that are involved in identifying the stimulus and organizing and initiating an appropriate response.

3. The time needed for the muscle systems to be activated and to carry out the response commanded.

Despite this apparent simplicity we expect to see a good deal of variability across subjects and within subjects in measured reaction times.

Procedure

You will sit at the computer looking at the screen at a distance of about 60cm (24") and will see a plus sign (+) in the centre of the screen. This is your *fixation point* or fixation spot and as you look at it, it will change rapidly to a circle (0), at the same position on the screen. The plus sign will stay on the screen for a different length of time on each occasion that it appears, before changing to the circle.

Your task as the subject is to press a key *as soon as the stimulus change occurs* (but remember to use the same key each time and also use the same finger each time, preferably the index finger of your dominant hand - usually the one you write with).

You will be given 3 trials (3 presentations of the stimulus change) as practice before you start the experiment itself which will consist of 20 trials. If you take longer than 1600 milliseconds (1.6 seconds) to respond, the computer will ignore your response and repeat the trial.

Simple Reaction Time

Results

The computer will display your reaction times for 20 trials and you should copy this information into Table 1.1.

Table 1.1. Reaction time data in milliseconds for a single subject across 20 trials.

Trial	RT
1	
2	
3	
4	
5	
6	
7	
8	
9	
10	
11	
12	
13	
14	
15	
16	
17	
18	
19	
20	

Now record: Your mean RT _____ milliseconds

and your range _____ - _____ milliseconds.

The computer will proceed to display a graph of your 20 trials as this will often give a clearer appreciation of response variation over trials. After this a *histogram* can be seen in which the test data from a large group of subjects is graphed.

The group mean RT is _____ milliseconds

and the group range is _____ - _____ milliseconds?

You should now proceed to make an approximate copy of the shape of the distribution into Fig. 1.1. Remember to mark any of the axes that do not provide all the necessary information. Just copy the axes' labels from the screen.

Simple Reaction Time

Fig. 1.1. *Frequency distribution of mean simple reaction times for a large group of subjects.*

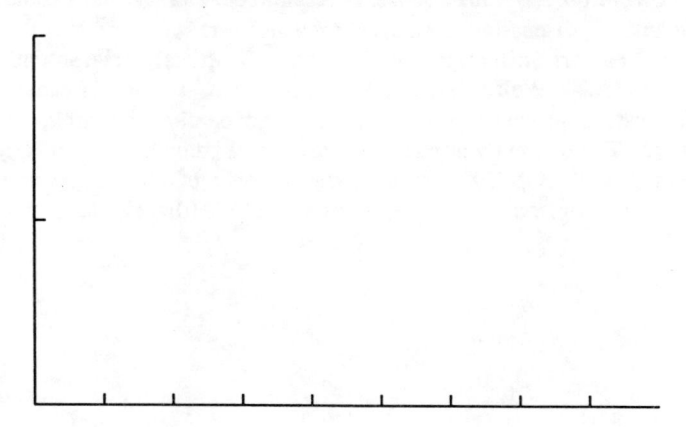

Discussion

We have included below a number of questions that you might like to think about in relation to the experiment which you have just completed.

You should now be able to appreciate the degree of intra-subject variability in even the simplest of tasks. Do you think that this variability will decrease with increasing practice and if so why?

Why do you think that the fixation point (plus sign) was presented for a different length of time on each trial before changing into a circle? How would your results differ if the time was constant?

If you wanted to keep reaction times low, do you think there might be an optimal time for the fixation point to remain on the screen before the stimulus onset? If so, do you think there may be practical, (e.g. industrial) applications for this psychological knowledge?

If you look again at the graph of the group data you will notice that the shape of the histogram is not symmetrical on either side of the most frequently obtained reaction time (the *mode*) with a sharp drop on the left as reaction times get shorter and a much more gradual decrease on the right as reaction times get longer. This can be restated as there being a greater spread of high scores than of low scores, which in statistical terms means that the data are *positively skewed*. Thinking about these skewed data, can you say why the computer was programmed to rerun trials where the latency was greater than 1.6 seconds and do you think that this has any implications for the *measure of central tendency* that we should adopt with reaction time data?

Would you have expected very short latencies to be more prevalent than suspiciously long latencies and why? Think of the terms *floor effect* and *ceiling effect*. Remember to refer back to your graph of the data distribution.

Why do you think that you were asked always to use the same button and the same finger?

In case you think that this type of research into subject variability is somewhat abstract, it is worth mentioning that many kinds of mental handicap caused by injury, disease or congenital abnormalities can potentially be diagnosed using reaction time measures. For example, most *psychopathological* conditions are associated with slower and more variable reaction times and a greater sensitivity to the various factors that normally influence reaction time (Nettlebeck, 1980).

References

Martindale, C. (1981). *Cognition and Consciousness*. Homewood: Dorsey. This book provides a thorough coverage of cognitive psychology, discussing mental chronometry in Chapter 4.

Nettlebeck, T. (1980). Factors affecting reaction time: Mental retardation, brain damage and other psychopathologies. In A.T. Welford (Ed.), *Reaction Times*. London: Academic. The book this chapter is drawn from is a most comprehensive coverage of reaction time research, but it is far too difficult to be sampled at this stage. Try it when you have a lot more background in psychology.

Posner, M.I. and Rogers, M.G.K. (1978). Chronometric analysis of abstraction and recognition. In W.K. Estes (Ed.), *Handbook of Learning and Cognitive Processes*, Vol.5. Hillsdale, N.J.: Lawrence Erlbaum Associates.

Notes

Notes

Chapter 2: Word Frequency and Recognition Speed

This unit is intended to provide an introduction to the use of scientific experiments in the study of mental processes through the medium of a basic experimental investigation. In the process, it is hoped to transmit some information about the way in which experiments are designed. There is no intention to provide a full alternative to a textbook on experimental design as this would be impossible in the space available. Readers are advised to consult one of the various texts on experimental design, several of which are referenced at the end of this unit (e.g. Christensen, 1980; Solso and Johnson, 1984). This unit will take the form of a description of an experiment together with a commentary on the design of this experiment. To make the distinction clearer, the experimental report and the commentary itself are printed in different fonts.

There is nothing magical about the methods of scientific enquiry. The essence of the scientific approach lies in conducting experiments in which one achieves a satisfactory level of *control*. This is arrived at through holding constant or in some way nullifying the influence of every important factor which you do not wish to measure and through the exact specification of each factor which you do wish to measure. The important problems are those involving the determination of which factors are likely to be important or relevant in any given situation and creating a method of experimentation which ensures that they are not allowed to influence the experimental results unduly.

In this unit, we are going to run an apparently simple experiment in an attempt to answer the question "Does the frequency of occurrence of a word in our language influence the speed with which we recognize that word?" and we are going to look at the design of a study which is intended to provide an answer. The best way for us to proceed is to use the standard experimental report layout to ensure that nothing is overlooked. When an experiment is published in a book or in a scientific journal, it is usually written in a standard format to allow other people to evaluate the way that the experiment has been run and to permit readers to re-run the experiment. You can make use of this format to help in the design-stage of your experiment. What we are going to do is to provide details of the various stages of a report and attempt to show how this process provides a useful way to ensure that you are systematic in producing a practical and effective experimental design. This first step is to state the basic ideas behind the experiment and this is followed by a systematic attempt to translate the reasons that we have for running the experiment into a workable experiment through the generation of a specific *hypothesis* which clearly sets out the prediction that we are making in terms of *independent variables* and *dependent variables*. This hypothesis is usually stated at the end of the introduction to the experiment. For the purposes of explaining the design procedure, we can state our hypothesis as follows:

The more common a word is to us, the faster we will recognize it.

Since it is rather difficult to look inside any individual's memory and say how common a particular word is for that person, we need a more objective hypothesis, such as:

The greater the frequency of occurrence of a word in its everyday use in our language, the faster that word will be recognized as being a word rather than a non-word.

As it is not logically possible to prove a hypothesis to be true, but only to show that a hypothesis cannot be true, we actually examine or test the obverse of the hypothesis, the null hypothesis, which in this case would probably be:

The frequency of occurrence of a word in everyday language has no effect on the speed of its recognition as being a word rather than a non-word.

The next stage is to provide operational definitions of the important terms in our null hypothesis. A variety of definitions are possible, but the following might be appropriate:

Independent variable – Frequency of occurrence of a word in everyday usage is defined as the number of times that a word has been counted as occurring in a survey of popular books and magazines, specifically that frequency recorded by Thorndike and Lorge (1944). Two levels of frequency will be examined – high (>100 occurrences per million words) and low (<10 occurrences per million words).

Word Frequency

> *Dependent variable – The speed with which a subject presses a button having decided that a tachistoscopically presented stimulus is a word rather than a non-word (i.e. a string of letters that do not form a word).*

This still leaves us plenty to think about. For example, what about *relevant variables*? Could the exact details of the method of stimulus presentation be a relevant variable? What about the words themselves, does it matter what the words are so long as they are of a given frequency? What about the subjects to be tested, how many should we test and does it matter what type of people they are? An experimenter has to be very systematic in answering these types of questions, similar examples of which are common to every experiment. We also have to consider what the experiment is going to measure. How do we measure *response speed*? We cannot simply show someone a word on a piece of paper and say, tell me when you recognize this. There is no easy way to measure how long it takes the subject to say yes I recognize this, nor is it possible to be sure that he is not cheating and simply saying that he recognises the word even if he does not. We therefore need to use equipment that will give us control over stimulus presentation and accurate measurement of response times relative to the time of presentation. For this purpose we could use a tachistoscope and timers, or more simply, a microcomputer. We can guard against cheating by giving the subject a task in which it will be obvious that he cannot guess successfully and if he does guess, his responses will balance out so that no effect will be found. A suitable task is one that is commonly used in the investigation of verbal processes. It involves the subject making a decision about whether or not a sequence of letters constitutes a word. Sometimes he will be presented with a letter-string that makes a word and sometimes the letter-string will not make up a word. The sequence of trials can be *randomized* so that it is not possible to predict what kind of stimulus will appear. This reduction of a task to a decision between only two possibilities is a frequently used technique in experimentation.

Introduction

This usually includes summaries of the important experiments that have already been carried out in the topic area under investigation and may include some coverage of the theoretical models that underlie work in the area. The types of experimental methods that have already been used and the specific design problems that have already been met and hopefully solved, will be discovered in the course of reading and summarizing this existing research.

The topic area with which we are concerned, involves the nature of our response to familiar words. Familiarity, of course, implies the operation of a memory system, since nothing can be familiar if there is no mechanism to tell us about our past experience. Indeed, human memory is the most pervasive aspect of human functioning since there is virtually nothing that we can do which does not involve at least some memory component. See if you can think of anything? Two principal types of memory have been identified – procedural and declarative. Procedural memory can be considered as memory for skills such as playing a musical instrument, riding a bicycle or solving a puzzle, while declarative memory is memory for facts such as your home telephone number or what your grandmother looks like. The memory system which we are to investigate is obviously declarative memory since we are interested in memory for words and how this memory affects the speed of a perceptual decision regarding such words.

Words have long been a principal focus of memory researchers, partly because language is so uniquely important a human attribute, and partly because words are so apparently simple to use as research material. The very earliest work attempted to make use of nonsense syllables such as CVC trigrams (e.g. JUB, PIB or TID because researchers wanted to avoid the possible contamination of specific experience with a word or words, on the operation of our memory (Ebbinghaus, 1885). However, it was soon realised that research with more natural stimuli was essential if an accurate representation of the operation of the memory system in natural contexts was to be obtained and the use of real words, sentences and stories became more common in research.

Once words were being used in memory research, it became obvious that the researchers who used nonsense syllables were at least partly justified in their distrust of real words, since words were found not to be equivalent to one another. It has been shown that words differ markedly in important attributes which affect a variety of things such as their rate of processing and their memorability. Amongst such attributes are factors like meaningfulness, pronounceableness, vividness and imagery. Meaningfulness is defined as the number of associations that can be drawn with the word in question. The more associates that can be generated by individuals with a word, the greater its meaningfulness is said to be (Noble, 1952). Noble found that words like ARMY and KITCHEN have a multitude of associations while words such as BODKIN and ULNA have few. Despite

Ebbinghaus' selection of nonsense syllables to avoid such pitfalls, it has been reported that even nonsense syllables have meaningful associations (Glaze, 1928), and these vary from many associations (e.g. BAL and ROV), to few (e.g. GUQ and ZIW). Pronounceableness is simply the ease with which a given word can be pronounced and has been examined in detail by Underwood and Schulz (1960). Vividness and imagery refer to the ease with which a word can elicit a visual image or mental picture, compare TANK with PITY in this respect (Paivio, 1965).

One of the more commonly addressed attributes of words is the objective frequency of occurrence, i.e. how often a word is encountered in written language. It has been suggested that the frequency of a word has a considerable influence on the way in which it is processed. The present experiment will examine the question, does the frequency of occurrence of a word in everyday usage affect the speed at which a subject can recognize that it is a word? It is possible that this type of enquiry may help to provide information about the way that the declarative memory system is designed.

Methods

This section is usually subdivided into the following parts:

i. Design

The purpose of this subsection is to ensure that the independent and dependent variables are specified as completely as possible and that the important details about the organization of the experiment are specified. For example, if there is more than one independent variable, are all subjects to be tested on all the independent variables or are different subjects to be tested on each? If the same subjects are to be tested on each, in what order will the different variables be tested? In our example, we have only one independent variable, but there are two *levels* of this variable (i.e. two *conditions*) - high frequency words and low frequency words. The best design would be to test the same subjects under the two conditions because this would ensure that the subjects tested in each condition would be comparable. In addition we should randomize the position or order in which the words are presented to the subjects so that we can control for any possible effect of word order. For example, we would not want to put all the low frequency words first, because subjects may get better at the experimental task with *practice* and this would bias the results towards producing faster response times from the later high frequency words. Alternatively subjects may be more attentive and motivated at the beginning of the experiment and therefore do better with the earlier test words. It should be noted that it may not always be possible to use a within subjects design, either for practical reasons or perhaps because there would be a likely *order effect* in which the running of a subject on one condition would influence his responses on a second condition. In this case a *between subjects* or perhaps a *mixed design* could be used.

Another design problem concerns what should be done about trials on which an error is made by the subject. Can we safely ignore these responses and analyse only the data from correct trials? Should we run additional trials to replace the trials on which errors were made?

This experiment will be a within subjects design in which the same subjects will be tested on both levels of a single independent variable - the frequency of occurrence of a word in everyday usage. This is defined as the number of times that a word has been counted as occurring in printed English in the published norms of Thorndike and Lorge (1944). Two levels of frequency will be examined - high and low. The dependent variable will be the speed with which a subject makes a decision that a tachistoscopically presented stimulus is a word rather than a non-word. The median response times will be used for the purpose of statistical analysis, with trials on which an error was made being repeated with different but equivalent stimuli and at a random point in the trial sequence until a correct response is made.

ii. Subjects

The number of subjects to be tested is important since some kinds of data analysis require a minimum number of subjects or require an equal number of subjects to be tested on different independent variables if comparisons are to be made between the results on each. The number of subjects to be tested should be the minimum necessary to show the desired effect, but you cannot simply test subjects one after the other and carry out an analysis of the results after each subject until you have the type of results that you are looking for. You have to decide on a *sample* size before running the study. In practice the number of subjects is often based on previous experience with similar studies and the underlying principle is that the stronger the effect under investigation, and the more *powerful* the test being applied, the fewer the subjects that will need to be tested. Are subjects to be volunteers or not, will this be

Word Frequency

important? Should they all be Caucasian, students, housewives, factory workers or a random sample of the population? What age and sex should they be? Do these factors really matter for the experiment in question? Obviously in some situations these things will matter a great deal, while in others they will not. Normally we might wish to test a fairly random sample of the general population in order to be sure of the generality of any effect measured, but this is rarely possible in real-life experimentation and probably not too important in many situations. On the other hand, it really must be borne in mind that most published results in Psychology have been and still are obtained from undergraduates in American universities.

The subjects in this experiment will be 14 undergraduate psychology students. The average age of the sample will be _____ , with 7 males and 7 females being tested. You will test yourself as one of these subjects and before you begin, you will be asked your age and sex so that the computer can calculate the average age of the subjects. The other 13 subjects will already have completed the experiment and you will be given their results after you have finished testing yourself.

iii. Stimuli

The actual stimuli need to be specified exactly. In our case we need to know the word frequency of course, but other factors must be taken into account. For example, the length of a word may be an important factor, because a long word may take longer to recognize than a short one. Coupled to this, long words could be found more often among less popular words (i.e. less frequent) than short words. If this were the case, any apparent effect of frequency may be attributable to word length instead. We can control for this by selecting words for each category of frequency in pairs, a five-letter word for the high frequency set and another five-letter word for the low frequency set and so on, with a third five-letter non-word being made up for the non-word condition. The number of words to be used has also to be decided. The greater the number of stimuli and therefore of trials, the less the effect of random factors is likely to be. However, against this must be counted the possible increase in boredom and tiredness as well as the decrease in motivation that are likely to occur with long experiments. A final point concerns the elimination of cheating through guessing which type of stimulus is going to appear. Subjects are very good at estimating the probability of occurrence of an event, so if there were twice as many word trials as non-word trials, then subjects would be biased in their responses towards the word decision. Obviously, therefore, there must be as many words as non-words.

This experiment will involve the presentation of 50 stimulus words, nouns that have been drawn from the Thorndike and Lorge (1944) word norms, with 25 in the high frequency category (less than 100 occurrences per million) and 25 in the low frequency category (less than 10 occurrences per million). The words in the two sets will be matched for word length. In addition, there will be 50 non-words, made up from the selected words by changing up to two letters from each word to create a pronounceable non-word. For example, if one of the test words was GRAPE, a suitable non-word would be GWATE. The order of occurrence of the words and the non-words will be randomized by the computer, a different random order being used for each subject. A further selection of 12 words and 12 non-words will be used as stimuli for a set of practice trials. In addition, there will be a pool of words meeting the above criteria so that when an error is made the trial can be repeated later with an equivalent stimulus. A fixation spot will also be used and this will take the form of a " * " in the centre of the screen.

iv. Apparatus/Procedure

How is each subject to be tested? What instructions will they be given about the task and how much should they know about what you expect to find? Instructions have to be clear and simple, otherwise your subject may not have a clue what is expected of him and his results will probably be completely useless. Do you need practice trials to make sure the subject is doing what he is supposed to and is performing to an acceptable standard? A further point to note is that psychologists have shown that the expectations of the experimenter can strongly influence the type of results that subjects produce. (This is at least partly the result of subjects trying to please the "powerful" experimenter. Sometimes known as the *Experimenter Effect*, this refers to the fact that the experimenter is often seen to be very important and powerful by the subject. As a result the subject tries hard to please the experimenter by doing exactly what he thinks the experimenter wants). What equipment is to be used and how will it be set up? Is the equipment safe, unobtrusive, and accurate, or is it unsafe, unreliable and inaccurate? You must not put subjects off with technological overkill, with wires leading everywhere and potentially lethal electrical equipment lying about waiting for its moment to produce a deceased subject or experimenter! Integrated microcomputers are now frequently used for many experiments because they are small, unobtrusive, powerful and accurate in controlling stimulus presentation and response recording.

The present experiment will involve each subject being tested singly. The subject will sit at the screen of a microcomputer and will read the instructions, equivalent to these, from the screen:

> You will sit facing the computer screen and you will be presented with a single stimulus by the computer. Your task is to decide if the stimulus is a word or is a string of letters which does not make up a word. You will indicate your response by pressing one of two keys on the computer keyboard, the " W " key for a Word decision and the " N " key for a Non-word decision.
>
> You will therefore at all times rest your left forefinger lightly over the " W " key on the keyboard and rest your right forefinger over the " N " key.
>
> When you are ready to begin the experiment itself, you will press the large SPACE BAR at the bottom of the keyboard. This will tell the computer that it is to start a trial. Each trial will begin with the computer asking you if you are ready. If you are, then press the SPACE BAR with your thumb. Almost immediately, a fixation spot in the form of a " * " will appear in the centre of the screen and this will be followed in a second or so by a string of letters. These letters will either be a word or a non-word. Decide as quickly as possible whether or not the stimulus is a word and press the correct key. However, while you must respond as quickly as possible, try not to make any mistakes. You will receive feedback on your responses: if you make a mistake the computer will "buzz"; if you respond too slowly you will hear a "beep-beep".
>
> Make sure you understand what you have to do? Read the instructions until you are quite sure about them.
>
> Once you are ready you should press the large SPACE BAR and the computer will give you some practice trials. Each practice trial will begin with the query, "READY?" to which you respond by pressing the SPACE BAR. The fixation spot and the stimulus will then appear in sequence. The actual experimental trials will follow on from the practice session.

Results

While it is true that the results can only appear after the experiment has been designed and run, it is no less true that no experiment should be designed without giving thought to the type of data which will be produced and the way in which that data will eventually be analyzed. Many researchers have completed large-scale and time-consuming testing of subjects only to find that there is no adequate way in which their data can be analysed. We have made sure that the data from this study can be simply and straightforwardly analyzed and this section covers the tabulation of the raw data produced by the experiment and the various manipulations that are carried out upon these data.

The first manipulation is usually to produce descriptive summaries of the data, which may take the form of summary tables and perhaps also graphs. Following this, the null hypothesis will usually be assessed through a comparison of the appropriate sets of figures by means of some kind of statistical test. Amongst the more frequently used of these tests are ones which compare two sets of scores (e.g. *t-tests*) and those which compare more than two sets (e.g. *Analysis of Variance*).

In this study, the computer will present your results as well as those of another 13 subjects and you should write this information very carefully into Table 2.1. Each figure represents the median time it took you to make a correct response in recognizing high and low frequency words. Your median non-word response time is also given.

Word Frequency

Table 2.1. *The effect of word frequency on the response speed of 14 subjects. The first 7 subjects are male, the second 7 are female.*

	Subject	High Frequency	Words Low Frequency	Non-words
	1	_____	_____	_____
	2	_____	_____	_____
	3	_____	_____	_____
	4	_____	_____	_____
	5	_____	_____	_____
	6	_____	_____	_____
You if Male	7	_____	_____	_____
	8	_____	_____	_____
	9	_____	_____	_____
	10	_____	_____	_____
	11	_____	_____	_____
	12	_____	_____	_____
	13	_____	_____	_____
You if Female	14	_____	_____	_____
	Group Mean	_____	_____	_____

The computer still has some additional information to provide which should be copied into Table 2.2.

Table 2.2. *Results of a correlated t-test.*

t	Degrees of freedom	Probability p
_____	_____	_____

This information will be discussed shortly. In the meantime you should calculate the arithmetic mean scores for all subjects on the low and the high frequency words and you should plot this information in the form of a line graph in Fig. 2.1. A sample set of values, 450 for Low Frequency, 500 for High Frequency and 550 for non-words has already been plotted as an example.

Fig. 2.1. Graph showing the effect of word frequency on word recognition time.

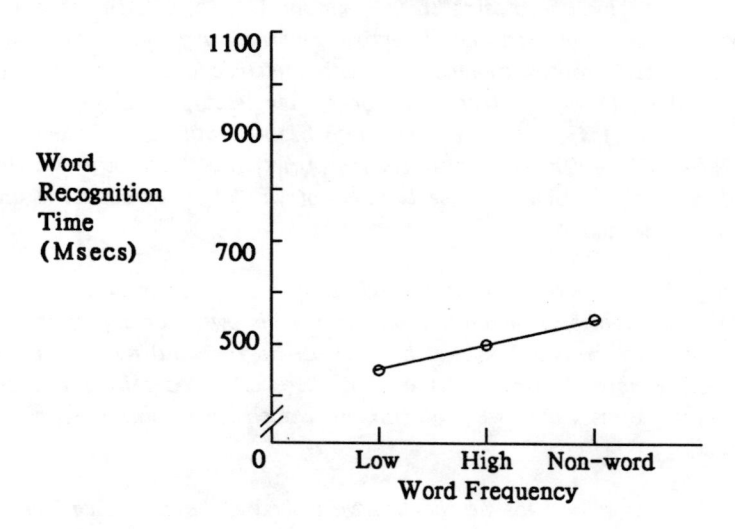

The next stage is for a statistical analysis to be computed in which the results from the high frequency words are compared with those from the low frequency words and with the non-words. The appropriate analysis when there are three sets of scores which are related because they have come from the same subjects would probably be an **Analysis of Variance**, *especially if we wanted to look at any differences in performance between the sexes. This is a little difficult to understand if you have never come across it before and therefore we will simplify our analysis in two ways. Firstly we will involve ourselves with only the comparison between high and low frequency words since it is these conditions which are directly referred to in our hypothesis. This allows us to use a simpler pairwise comparison test. Secondly, in order to simplify the computational aspect, the computer has carried out this analysis for you, but you should refer to an introductory statistics textbook for background information because you will have to perform similar analyses in other units. The actual test that is being employed is the* **matched-pairs t-test** *or* **t-test for correlated means** *in which the scores obtained by a sample of subjects on one part of the study (high frequency words) is compared with the scores from those same subjects obtained on a different part of the study (low frequency words). The computer has already given you the value of* **t**, *together with the* **degrees of freedom** *and the* **probability** *of obtaining that value of t purely by chance. You have previously recorded this in Table 2.2. If the* **probability (p)** *of getting a t-value as large as the one that you obtained is equal to or less than 5% (p<0.05), i.e. is the same as or is a smaller number than 5% or 0.05, then it is customary to accept that there is a real difference between the sets of scores that are being compared. If this difference is accepted as a real one and not some chance difference, then we must reject our null hypothesis that there is no difference between recognition time for high and low frequency words and thus we can support the hypothesis that recognition time for high frequency words is faster than for low frequency words.*

Discussion

The discussion section exists for the researcher to give meaning to the results he has obtained from the experiment, to relate his findings to those of previous researchers and to existing theories or models. It is also common for problems with the design, the materials or the conduct of the experiment to be discussed and ways suggested to get round existing shortcomings in future work. In addition, it is usual for the researcher to say how the described experimental work should be continued to provide further valuable information within the topic area.

In the present study, it is likely that you have obtained results which have allowed you to reject the null hypothesis. The implication of these results is that the declarative memory system is organized in such a way that the more readily occurring words can be accessed more rapidly than less frequently occurring words. This implies that words are not stored in the mind in the same way as they are in a dictionary or in a computer database, where it should be as easy to find one word as any other. The organization of human memory may therefore be said to be intelligently organized in that items which are more often needed are more easily available.

However, you may still wish to point out criticisms of the study itself. For example, there is a basic flaw in the study in that we cannot be sure if word frequency actually affects recognition time by itself or whether it is directly related to another factor which is causing the recognition time effect. In other words, word frequency may not really be independent of other attributes of verbal materials? Frincke (1968) carried out an analysis which suggested that frequency, and pronounceableness are both contained within the attribute meaningfulness and therefore frequency may not be the real effective factor in our study, it may be the underlying variable meaningfulness that matters. Other major attributes that have been identified as independent are imagery and pleasantness (Toglia and Battig, 1978). Did we control for the operation of these other variables? Would it be safe to assume that they would be fairly equal across the two sets of words? If we cannot assume this, what are the implications for the validity of this study?

We might also wish to consider the extent to which objective word frequency reflects the actual subjective frequency within each subject's experience and therefore within his own memory system. Can we be sure that there is a close relationship between the two. You may have noted that the word norms that we have used are quite old, being published in 1944. It is quite likely that even if there is a good relationship between objective and subjective frequency, the actual norms which we are using are inadequate because they no longer reflect current usage of the English language.

Could we have made more of our data? Perhaps we should have looked at the error data from the study to establish if more errors were made in one condition than another. In experiments which involve reaction times, it is essential that you check to make sure that there very few errors (certainly they should occur on less than 10% of trials) and that these errors are not more frequent in the conditions with the faster reaction times. The reason for this is the possibility of **speed-accuracy trade-off** *occurring, where the subject responds faster at the expense of more errors. You could call this the quick-and-careless response and if it occurs in only one condition can obviously upset the experimental results.*

Another thing that has not been mentioned, but which is an essential part of sound experimental practice, is the process of debriefing, which refers to the system of asking each subject for his own subjective interpretation of what happened in the experiment, what problems he experienced and any criticisms that he has. This may well shed light on unsuspected difficulties with the design, the stimuli or the equipment. In addition, it is ethically necessary to tell the subject what the experiment was about in sufficient detail for him to feel that there was some point to the exercise.

Recommended Reading

Carlson, N.R. (1984). *Psychology*. Boston: Allyn and Bacon. (Chapter 2).
Roediger, H.L., Rushton, J.P., Capaldi, E.D., and Paris, S.G. (1984). *Psychology*. Boston: Little, Brown. (Pages 19-33).

References

Christensen, L.B. (1980). *Experimental Methodology*. Boston: Allyn and Bacon.
Cohen, L., and Holliday, M. (1982). *Statistics for Social Scientists*. London: Harper and Row.
Ebbinghaus, H.E. (1885). Uber das Gedachtuis. Leipzig: Dunker. Translated as *Memory*, (C.E. Bussenius, Translator), New York: Teachers' College, 1913.
Frincke, G. (1968). Word characteristics, associative-relatedness, and the free-recall of nouns. *Journal of Verbal Learning and Verbal Behavior, 7,* 366-372.
Glaze, J.A. (1928). The association value of nonsense syllables. *Journal of Genetic Psychology, 35,* 255-269.
Greene, J., and D'Oliveira, M. (1982). *Learning to use Statistical Tests in Psychology*. London: Harper and Row.
Hall, J.F. (1982). *An Invitation to Learning and Memory*. Boston: Allyn and Bacon.
Noble, C.E. (1952). The analysis of meaning. *Psychological Review, 59,* 421-430.

Noble, C.E. (1953). The meaning-familiarity relationship. *Psychological Review, 60,* 89-98.

Paivio, A. (1965). Abstractness, imagery, and meaningfulness in paired-associate learning. *Journal of Verbal Learning and Verbal Behavior, 4,* 32-38.

Solso, R.L., and Johnson, H.H. (1984). *An Introduction to Experimental Design in Psychology: A Case Approach.* New York: Harper and Row.

Thorndike, E.L., and Lorge, I. (1944). *The Teacher's Word Book of 30,000 Words.* New York: Columbia University.

Toglia, M.P., and Battig, W.F. (1978). *Handbook of Semantic Word Norms.* Hillsdale, N.J.: Lawrence Erlbaum Associates.

Underwood, B.J., and Schulz, R.W. (1960). *Meaningfulness and Verbal Learning.* Philadelphia: Lippincott.

Word Frequency

Notes

Chapter 3 : Waterfall Effect

Much of the work that has been carried out into the way that our visual systems operate has had a strong neurophysiological background. The main reason for this has been the belief that the best way to comprehend vision is to gain an adequate understanding of the structure of the visual system and its operation at the level of the individual cell or small cell groups. Can you name any of the types of cell associated with the visual system?

This research represents an orientation towards the machinery of the visual system rather than the processes that such machinery carries out. Much of the impetus for this work came from Hubel and Wiesel (1959, 1968) who were awarded the Nobel Prize for their pioneering efforts. The main conclusions that can be derived from this work is that it is possible to say with a degree of accuracy that the process of visual perception involves taking visual input and breaking it down into certain components, each of which will be analysed by a different structure (grouping of specialized cells) within the brain. The outputs from the processing of these various components may then be synthesized into a "whole" again.

The way that this type of *neurophysiological* work is carried out generally involves surgical work with animals in which very small *microelectrodes* are inserted into the brain and into the centre of a single cell. Such an electrode can be attached to an instrument to measure the electrical activity of the cell in which it is inserted. It has been known for some time that even when brain cells are not actually doing anything in the way of handling incoming information, they fire (give off an electrical discharge) spontaneously at a rate that can be measured. However, when they are receiving an input from the senses, the rate of firing will increase considerably. Therefore by measuring the electrical activity of each individual cell by means of the microelectrode, while presenting a variety of types of stimulus to the eye, it is possible to find out which type of stimulus causes the largest increase in neural firing rate. This stimulus could well be the stimulus for which that cell is designed to respond. For example, Hubel and Wiesel found cells which responded only to lines of a particular length and width, at a particular orientation (e.g. vertical) and then only when the line appeared at a particular place on the *retina*. Other cells have been found that respond only to the colour of a stimulus and still others that respond only to movement (Mollon, 1974).

Some confirmation of the results from microelectrode research (*neuroelectrophysiological recording*) has been provided by research using *radioactive dyes* such as 2-deoxyglucose. These substances can be injected into the brain and will be taken-up selectively by cells which are active at a particular time. Thus, the dye is injected at the same time as a particular type of visual stimulus is presented to the subject. Those cells which are most involved in handling the type of stimulus information that is being received will take some of the dye into their bodies. The subject is then killed (*sacrificed*), the brain removed, prepared in special fluids, and then cut into thin slices for viewing under a microscope under special light. This light will allow the scientist to find those cells in the brain that contain the dye and thus to pinpoint the active cell locations.

As far as extending this work to humans is concerned, there are, as you may already have realised, some potential problems. The techniques require that subjects have holes bored in their skulls and electrodes inserted, and possibly that they be sacrificed and have their brains sliced up for analysis. Perhaps unsurprisingly, there are few human volunteers (despite offering subjects small but worthwhile financial inducements). As a result, research into human vision can only be extrapolated from other animals, (most work has been done on the cat and on the monkey) or carried out by very indirect methods. Amongst these indirect methods can be found the study of *after-effects*, called by some "the psychologist's microelectrode" (Frisby, 1979). After-effects are visual illusions which are generally experienced only after a fairly prolonged exposure to a particular type of stimulus. Perhaps the most common after-effect is that experienced after one has been looking at a bright source of light such as a flash-bulb or the sun. What is experienced afterwards is an image of the original light source which can be seen at the same time as the scene which is being looked at currently. Can you describe any other after-effects which you have experienced and which are not mentioned in this chapter?

Most after-effects are *negative after-effects* in that they are experienced as the opposite of the original stimulus. Thus, if we stare at a patch of green card for a few minutes and then look at a grey card, we will see the grey card as red for some time (in colour vision, red and green are, in an important sense, opposites). Why do such after-effects occur? The most commonly expressed explanation is couched in terms of neural fatigue, that is, when cells which handle a particular type of information (e.g. the colour green) are *adapted* (exposed for a long period) to that information, they get "tired" and gradually reduce their capacity to fire in response. The output of the visual system is then unbalanced and other cells (e.g. red colour cells) appear to respond more strongly because they are no longer being counterbalanced by the adapted cells. The experience in our example, is of seeing more red than we would otherwise have done in a grey stimulus which should contain all colours in roughly equal amounts. If this

Waterfall Effect

an acceptable explanation, one can see why Mollon (1974) said "if it adapts, it is there" (p. 479), since the very fact that you can induce a particular after-effect indicates that there must be neural cells which specialize in the type of information concerned.

What are the principal visual after-effects? In fact, after-effects have been found with brightness, colour, shape, tilt, size, and motion, as well as being found with other sensory systems. The one that we are going to consider in this module is that of motion, the motion after-effect or MAE. Can you describe an after-effect from a sensory system other than vision?

Instructions to Subjects

There will be three trials. For each trial you should sit about 45 to 60 cms (18 to 24 ins) away from the screen. During each trial you will be shown a pattern which will flow vertically across the screen in a continuous fashion. Your task is to gaze at the middle of the screen for the full 3 minutes that the moving pattern is shown . While the moving pattern is being shown you should attempt as well as you can to keep looking at the centre of the screen. Do your best not to track the lines with your eyes and try to keep your head still.

After 3 minutes the computer will "beep" and the pattern will stop moving. You should keep your gaze fixated on the screen. If the experiment works with you then you will experience the sensation that the pattern is drifting either in the same or in the opposite direction to the original movement (even though you know that it is motionless). Eventually this impression of drift will disappear. We want to know when that happens. That is, the pattern will move for 3 minutes, then it will stop. At that point it may seem to drift for some time. When you are reasonably sure that it has stopped drifting you should indicate this by pressing the space-bar on the keyboard. Some people get the drifting sensation for minutes and some don't get it at all - so don't worry if either it seems to last a long time or if you don't experience it even slightly.

For each trial, you will be asked to view the pattern with either a particular eye or with both eyes when the pattern is moving and to view the stationary pattern either with the same eye or a different eye or both. The computer will tell you which eye-combination to use before each trial begins - make a note in the space provided below. You should pay close attention to this information as you have to remember whether to change eyes or not when the pattern stops moving. You either close the eye you are not using or cover it with your hand.

There will be a 5-minute rest between trials. You may have a rest during this period, perhaps even close your eyes.

After each trial, i.e. when the drifting has stopped and you have pressed the space bar, you may like to jot down any interesting observations in the space provided below. At the end the computer will present a set of results. Copy these into Table 3.1.

Table 3.1.   *Information regarding the three trials in the present experiment.*

Trial 1 :   Eye used for moving pattern :   LEFT / RIGHT / BOTH
            Eye used for stationary pattern: LEFT / RIGHT / BOTH

Observations:

_____

_____

_____

_____

Waterfall Effect

Trial 2 : Eye used for moving pattern : LEFT / RIGHT / BOTH
Eye used for stationary pattern: LEFT / RIGHT / BOTH

Observations:
_____
_____
_____
_____

Trial 3 : Eye used for moving pattern : LEFT / RIGHT / BOTH
Eye used for stationary pattern: LEFT / RIGHT / BOTH

Observations:
_____
_____
_____
_____

AT THIS POINT YOU SHOULD READ NO FURTHER, BUT CARRY ON AND RUN YOURSELF AS A SUBJECT.

Waterfall Effect

The motion after-effect (MAE) can be readily experienced in a variety of forms outside the laboratory. For example, when you have been driving along in a car while looking at the road surface and the car comes to a halt, the car can appear to roll backwards a little or the ground to move forwards. More commonly experienced, however, is the effect which follows staring at a waterfall for a period of time. If you look away at the bank of the river, you will often experience an effect of the bank rising upwards. This is why the MAE is often referred to as the Waterfall Effect. In the laboratory, a common way to examine MAE's is to use a rotating spiral which can produce a very strong MAE (*Spiral After-effect*).

What can we assume about the visual system from a discovery that the waterfall after-effect exists? The first thing we can say is that there most probably are cells in the visual system which respond primarily or entirely to movement and that this responsiveness is to movement in one direction only. Thus when the visual system experiences movement in a given direction, this information is detected and signalled by a particular set of visual cells which respond to that direction of movement. Once these cells adapt, their output in no-signal conditions, i.e. when there is no movement present is temporarily reduced. The system is then out of balance and the resting firing-rate of the other cells is greater with the result that the interpretation is made of perceiving movement in the opposite direction. See Fig. 3.1 for a visual representation of the effect. The arrows represent the firing rates of cells responsive to movement in four *orthogonal* directions. The eye termed the non-adapted eye is looking at a stationary stimulus and all four cells are firing at the same rate (e.g. 10 units per sec) and so the perception is of a stationary scene. The same eye, once it has been looking at a moving display, is termed the adapted eye. It has been viewing downward movement so the 'downward' receptor is adapted and reduces its firing rate by half to 5 units. The opposite 'upward' receptor now outweighs the 'downward' receptor and upward movement is signalled and subjectively perceived. After a short time, the adaptation level of the 'downward' receptor decays and the two receptors come back into balance and the visual scene stabilizes. The greater the period of adaptation, the longer this will take to happen.

Fig. 3.1. *A graphical representation of the effect of adaptation to downward movement on the perception of upward movement when the eye is viewing a stationary scene.*

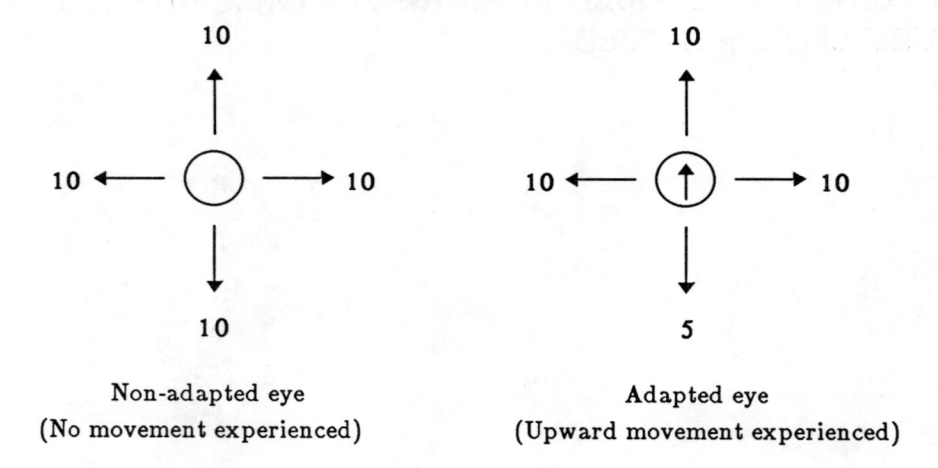

Non-adapted eye
(No movement experienced)

Adapted eye
(Upward movement experienced)

Rationale for the Experiment
We have talked about the MAE indicating the existence of movement-sensitive cells (motion detectors) in the visual system, but we have not said just where in the visual system these cells might be found. One possibility is that movement-sensitive cells are to be found in the retina itself or it may be that they are to be found in more central structures such as the visual cortex in the brain itself. See Fig. 3.2 for a simplified diagram of the visual system.

Fig.3.2. *Diagram of the visual system showing the primary pathway from Retina to Visual Cortex via the Lateral Geniculate Nucleus (LGN) and the secondary connections with the mid-brain.*

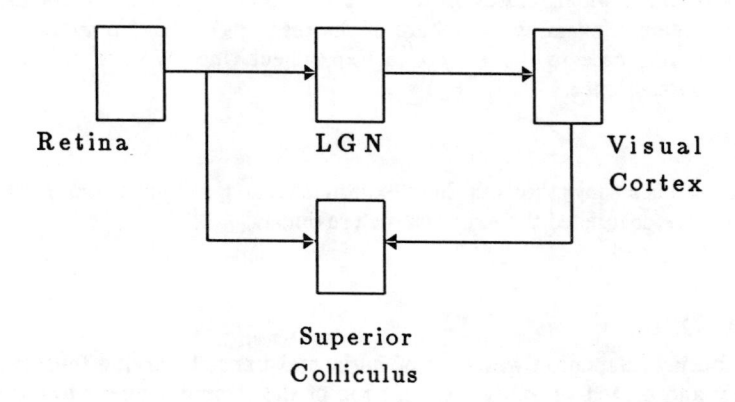

Retina → LGN → Visual Cortex

Superior Colliculus

How might we examine these possibilities? One way to do this, is to see if the MAE will show inter-ocular transfer. That is, when we use only one eye during adaptation (monocular viewing), can the MAE be demonstrated when the other non-adapted eye views a stationary stimulus? If it cannot, this could be taken to be evidence that the retina is the source of the effect which is not transferring to parts of the brain to which the other eye is connected. If the MAE can be demonstrated in the other eye, it suggests that the effect is of more central origin. This is the experiment that is being examined in this chapter as we are assessing the extent of interocular transfer of the MAE. The main experiment is designed to show that the effect is not simply the result of fatigue in the retinal receptors for motion, but has a central component. The second experiment represents a demonstration of the strength of the illusory movement and the independence of the motion percept of other evidence which indicates no movement.

Design
a) Experiment One:

The main experiment concerned the results obtained from Trials 1 and 2. The independent variable in the main experiment was the viewing condition which was in effect during adaptation and after-effect testing. Two levels were used:

1) Monocular – Adapt to a waterfall stimulus with right eye only for 180 seconds. Test the duration of the MAE with the right eye only and a static stimulus.

2) Interocular – Adapt to a waterfall stimulus with the right eye only for 180 seconds. Test the duration of the MAE with the left eye only and a static stimulus.

For half the subjects the monocular condition preceded the interocular condition, the remaining subjects experiencing the interocular condition first.

The dependent variable was the subject's estimate of the duration of the after-effect, coupled with information regarding the direction of the after-effect. Since subjects will occasionally report a positive after-effect, i.e. where the experience of movement is in the same direction as that experienced during adaptation, direction must be taken into account. The easiest way to accomplish this is to give each value of the duration of the after-effect a sign which corresponds to the direction of the perceived after-effect. Thus if the MAE is in the expected upward direction, the estimate of duration will be given a positive value, but if it is downwards, it will be given a negative value. For example, a perceived upwards MAE lasting 120 seconds would be recorded as +120, while a perceived downwards MAE lasting 25 seconds would be recorded as −25.

Waterfall Effect

b) Experiment Two:

The final trial, Trial 3, constituted a demonstration providing the opportunity for both eyes to view, during adaptation, a waterfall stimulus which moves in opposite directions on either half of the screen. Both eyes then viewed the stationary stimulus to examine the nature of the resulting MAE. No attempt will be made to relate the duration of the effect in this case to the effects in Experiment One. We are just interested in the subjective interpretation of the MAE experience.

Subjects

You will have run yourself as a subject in both these experiments and will have been provided with the data from a further 13 subjects who have completed the experiments previously.

Stimuli

a) Experiment One:

The stimulus display during adaptation was a set of horizontal lines of varying thickness and length which were introduced successively and moved smoothly from the top of the computer screen to the bottom of the screen. The subjective impression is usually of a pattern flowing down the screen in a smooth and steady fashion. The test stimulus was the identical display frozen on the screen.

b) Experiment Two:

The stimulus display was identical to that used in Experiment One with the exception that while the left half of the stimulus display moved smoothly upwards, the right half moved downwards. The test stimulus was the same display frozen on the screen.

Procedure

The procedure for each of the experiments has been outlined in some detail in the Instructions to Subjects.

Results

a) Experiment One:

The computer has already provided estimates of the duration of the MAE's for you and 13 other subjects and you should have copied this information into Table 3.2. You should now calculate the mean MAE duration for each condition of viewing, fill the information into the last line of Table 3.2 and plot these means for Experiment One as a line graph in Fig. 3.3. Provide a suitable scale for the Y-axis (the vertical line) which does not necessarily start at zero and which makes the most of any difference in time between the two conditions. Write this information next to the axis.

Waterfall Effect

Table 3.2. *The duration of the MAE in seconds, under three conditions of viewing.*

	Experiment 1		Experiment 2
Subject	Monocular	Interocular	Binocular
1	_____	_____	_____
2	_____	_____	_____
3	_____	_____	_____
4	_____	_____	_____
5	_____	_____	_____
6	_____	_____	_____
7	_____	_____	_____
8	_____	_____	_____
9	_____	_____	_____
11	_____	_____	_____
12	_____	_____	_____
13	_____	_____	_____
You	_____	_____	_____
Group Mean	_____	_____	_____

Fig. 3.3. *A line graph of the MAE duration under two different viewing conditions.*

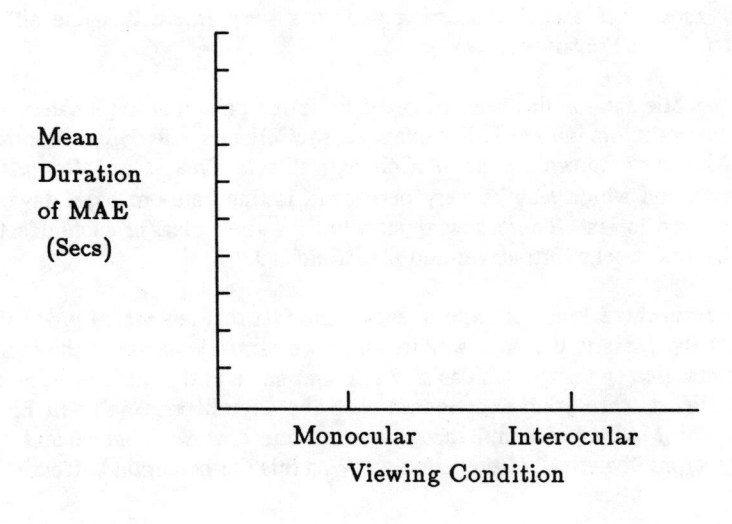

Mean Duration of MAE (Secs)

Monocular   Interocular
Viewing Condition

Express the duration of the MAE under interocular viewing as a % of the duration of the MAE under monocular viewing. Your estimate of this is: _____ %?

Waterfall Effect

If we wanted to be sure that there was a real difference between the set of times under monocular viewing and those under interocular viewing, we would usually need to carry out a suitable statistical test. With the data that we have, it would probably be appropriate to use a matched-pairs t-test (t-test for correlated means). The procedure for calculating this test is explained in a later chapter and you may wish to return to this data set to carry out the t-test at a later date. (If our data did not satisfy the requirements of a parametric test, a suitable non-parametric equivalent would be the *Wilcoxon Test*). It is quite probable, however, that the differences that you have found are so large that there could be little doubt about there being a real difference between the two sets of scores. For example, if you found the same direction of effect for every or nearly every subject, i.e. all the subjects reported longer MAE's in the monocular condition, then you could be quite confident in your results. Another possible statistical analysis would be to use a *Sign Test* to see if the number of subjects experiencing a negative after-effect was significantly greater than the number experiencing a positive after-effect.

b) Experiment Two:

This was a demonstration and requires no data analysis other than a consideration of the subjective comments made after completing Trial 3. Reference to this will be made at the end of the Discussion.

Discussion

Although not all experimenters have actually found interocular transfer (Pickersgill and Jeeves, 1958), you will probably have found in Experiment One that the longer MAE's were reported in the monocular condition and that the average duration under interocular conditions was only about half as long. What do you think this means?

Gregory (1966) argues that the MAE is too complex a phenomena to be the sole responsibility of the retina, but he feels that this type of experiment that we have carried out does not prove conclusively that the retina is not the responsible agent. He points out that it is possible that even when the adapted eye is closed during the test period with the other eye, it may still be sending information that affects the responses of the tested eye. This may be the case, although it does indicate that there must be a central aspect to the effect because the two eyes are only linked in the cortex itself where retinal cells project to *binocular cells*.

Favreau (1975) has carried out an important set of studies which bear on these issues. Her main conclusions are that there are two components to the MAE, one of which is fairly short lasting and is the result of the operation of binocularly driven cells (i.e. visual cells which receive their input from both eyes) and the other of which is more persistent and is the result of the operation of monocularly driven cells. The first set of cells she hypothesizes to lie in a part of the mid-brain known as the *superior colliculus* which appears to be specialized for processing movement information and for guiding eye-movements (See Fig. 3.2). The second set of cells she locates in the visual cortex itself where the specialization is more concerned with form or shape perception. This kind of distinction between the visual cortex and the superior colliculus is one that has been made by many other researchers regarding other aspects of visual processing and is a very interesting one although it is often too simplistically stated (Bronson, 1974; Trevarthen, 1968).

It also requires mention that while fatigue has been reported to be the principal explanation of after-effects, it is also possible that there are other factors involved. For example, McCollough (1965) has reported the existence of a *contingent after-effect* (CAE), now known as the McCollough effect. This is an after-effect which seems to depend on associative learning and which may be very persistent, lasting hours or even days, certainly far longer than mere cell fatigue is believed to last. There now appears to be a whole class of such effects and at least one of these appears to persist for up to 6 weeks (Stromeyer and Mansfield, 1970).

What is demonstrably clear from these kinds of experiments is the fact that our visual processing is carried on at a number of levels simultaneously. This is the only way in which we can make sense of the fact that it is possible to see the same stimulus do contradictory things, such as stay still and move at the same time, or move simultaneously in two opposite directions. What were your experiences with the stimuli, especially in Experiment Two? The normally reported effect of the MAE is of simultaneous upward and downward movement of the static stimulus which is resolved into an apparent "twisting" of the stimulus. Was this the perceptual effect that you experienced?

Recommended Reading
Gregory, R.L. (1966) *Eye and Brain*. London: Weidenfeld and Nicolson. (Chapter 7).

References
Bronson, G.W. (1974). The postnatal growth of visual capacity. *Child Development, 45,* 873-890.

Favreau, O.E. (1976). Motion aftereffects: Evidence for parallel processing in motion perception. *Vision Research, 16,* 181-186.

Frisby, J.P. (1979). *Seeing: Illusion, Brain and Mind.* Oxford: Oxford University.

Hubel, D.H., and Wiesel, T.N. (1959). Receptive fields of single neurones in the cat's striate cortex. *Journal of Physiology, 148,* 574-591.

Hubel, D.H., and Wiesel, T.N. (1968). Receptive fields and functional architecture of monkey striate cortex. *Journal of Physiology, 195,* 215-243.

Mayhew, J.E.W., and Anstis, S.W. (1972). Movement after-effects contingent on colour, intensity and pattern. *Perception and Psychophysics, 12,* 77-85.

McCollough, C. (1965). The conditioning of color perception. *American Journal of Psychology, 78,* 362-368.

Mollon, J. (1974). After-effects and the brain. *New Scientist, 61,* 479-482.

Pickersgill, M.J., and Jeeves, M.A. (1958). After-effects of movement produced by a rotating spiral. *Nature, 182,* 1820.

Stromeyer, C.F., and Mansfield, R.J.W. (1970). Colored after-effects produced with moving edges. *Perception and Psychophysics, 2,* 108-114.

Trevarthen, C.B. (1968). Two mechanisms of vision in primates. *Psychologische Forschung, 31,* 299-337.

Notes

Chapter 4: Muller-Lyer Illusion

One major area of psychology has been the study of the *sensory* and *perceptual* systems. Scientists have been concerned with these systems because they are of great intrinsic interest, but also because the study of sensation and perception can tell us much about the way in which the mind organizes our experiences and therefore provides clues regarding the processes which are carried out in the brain. Of all our senses, the visual system has received the most attention and is perhaps the most difficult to comprehend. It is probably no accident that an estimated 60% of the human brain is dedicated to visual processing.

When students first give thought to how the visual system actually works, they frequently use a television camera system as an analogy. However, the human visual system is not a passive data recorder like a camera. The eye and its associated visual structures are actually an extension of the brain, an extension which actively processes the information received. Consider a situation in which you are running along a street. The world will appear relatively stable and fixed as you run through it. Now think of documentary films that you have seen in which a hand-held camera is carried at speed through a scene. What do you remember? Was the view experienced not chaotic, with the scene jumping and shaking about in an alarming fashion? This is one example of the way in which the visual system continually attempts to present the visual world as it really is and not as it may momentarily appear and other striking examples can be seen in the *perceptual constancies*. The study of the veridical nature of visual processing has indicated the considerable dependence of perception upon existing knowledge about the world. Thus when we have to recognize a visual form in the sky, we do not require to "consider" objects that would not normally be found there, such as double-decker buses. This simplification of the processing task we can call *contextual facilitation*.

However, the visual system does not always operate in a veridical manner and this can be demonstrated with many visual *illusions*. Rather than simply cataloguing such instances of non-veridical perception and forgetting about them, many psychologists have studied them in detail. The reason for this is that examining situations where the visual system does not provide a truthful interpretation of the world might provide a doorway through which we can peek to discover something about normal veridical perception. Three of the more common illusions are illustrated in Fig. 4.1, and the explanation of each may tell us much about the way our visual apparatus must function.

Fig. 4.1. *Examples of (a) the Ponzo, (b) the Poggendorff and (c) the Titchener illusions.*

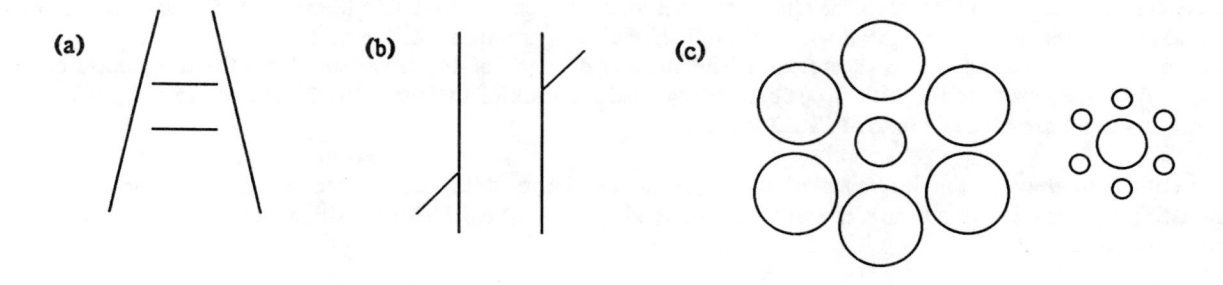

Perhaps the most studied of all illusions, however, is the Muller-Lyer illusion which is illustrated in Fig.4.2.

Fig. 4.2. *Illustration of the most common form of the Muller-Lyer illusion.*

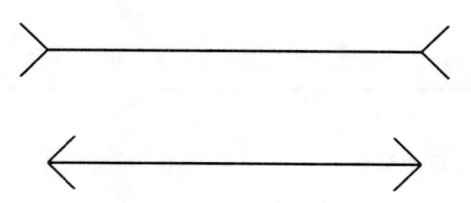

Muller-Lyer

In this illusion, the line with the arrowheads going outwards, appears to be longer than the line with the arrowheads going inwards. The strength of this illusion can be affected to some extent by several factors and in this experiment we will examine the possible influence of the angle at which the arrowheads meet the lines.

Design

This experiment will be run using a *within subjects* design in which each subject will be tested under each condition of the study. How else do you think we might have designed the study? The *independent variable* is the angle of the arrowheads to the vertical, with 5 levels of this variable being used (0, 15, 30, 45 and 60 degrees of angle). The *dependent variable* is the magnitude of the illusion effect assessed by the *method of adjustment*. In this method, the lengths of the two lines are adjusted until they are judged to be subjectively equal to each other. When this occurs, each line should be 100 units in length, the units being arbitrary measures on the screen. The physical difference in length between the two lines is then measured and expressed as a percentage:

$$\frac{\text{Length of Arrow In line} - \text{Length of Arrow Out line}}{2}$$

There are a number of *relevant* extraneous variables which will have to be taken into account. For example, it is known that the magnitude of the Muller-Lyer effect is to some extent a function of the amount of exposure to the figures. Therefore it is important that the figures are looked at for as short a time as possible. This problem will be one experienced in a within subjects design as an *order effect* and the influence of such effects must be controlled. One way to do this is to *counterbalance* the order in which examples of the 5 levels of angle are tested:

$$0, 15, 30, 45, 60, 60, 45, 30, 15, 0$$

However, we shall use a *randomization* procedure in which each subject in the experiment will receive examples of each angle (5 options) in a randomly determined sequence selected by the computer. To prevent any influence of effects such as the direction in which the arrowhead is to be moved or on which side the Out and In arrowheads are shown, these factors will be counterbalanced so that on half of all the trials the Out Arrow will be shown on the left of the figure, and on half the trials the Out Arrow will be shown on the right side (2 options). For each of these 10 (5 x 2) options the middle arrowhead will begin in half the trials on the left of the centre of the line and in half the trials on the right of the centre (2 options). The starting distance of the arrowhead from the true centre of the figure will vary across trials, with 3 positions being used for each of the foregoing 20 options (5 x 2 x 2). This means that there are 60 trials in total (5 x 2 x 2 x 3).

In addition, to prevent the influence of the edges or the centre of the screen providing a reference point for estimating the centre of the figure, the whole stimulus will appear at a different position (set of coordinates) on the screen on every trial.

Stimuli

As previously stated, there will be 12 examples of each of the 5 angles of figure, making 60 stimuli in total and they will be presented on the computer screen in the form of the combined Muller-Lyer figure, as depicted in Fig. 4.3.

Fig. 4.3. *Example of a combined Muller-Lyer stimulus figure with arrowheads at 45 degrees from the vertical.*

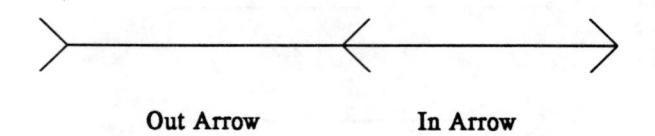

Procedure

Your task as the subject is to sit at the computer and to look at the centre of the screen. When you are ready, you will press the large SPACE BAR on the keyboard, at which point the first figure will be presented on the screen. The central arrowhead in the figure will be either to the left or to the right of centre (the actual direction and distance from centre being selected at random by the computer) and your task is to move this central arrowhead until it appears to you to be in the centre so that the lines on either side of it appear to be equal in length.

Remember, do not try to compensate for the illusion effect, *judge as you see*. After all, we are trying to measure the size of an illusion, not your ability to cope with an illusion.

You can move the central arrowhead by pressing either the --> key to make it go right or the <-- key to make it go left. Press these keys as often as you like, but the first press will make the central arrowhead move in the direction of the key and it will keep moving in that direction until you press the SPACE BAR to stop it, or you press the other direction key when it will change direction. If you reach the end of the figure, just press the opposite direction key and the arrowhead will move back toward the centre. Try to make your judgment quickly since you know the amount of time you spend looking at the figure will reduce the strength of any effect. Once you have actually decided on your judgment, press the RETURN key to let the computer know your decision.

Sit for a moment, relax, look at the centre of the screen and then press the SPACE BAR to see the next stimulus figure.

Results

After you have made 60 judgments, the computer will present your results, which will be in the form of percentage errors. You should copy this information accurately into Table 4.1. After you have done this, the computer will present the *median* data from 9 subjects who have already completed this experiment. Copy this information carefully into Table 4.2 and add your own median data from Table 4.1 as the 10th subject.

Table 4.1. *Differences between the Out and In Arrow lengths (i.e. % Error).*

Degree of Angle from Vertical

Trial	0	15	30	45	60
1	___	___	___	___	___
2	___	___	___	___	___
3	___	___	___	___	___
4	___	___	___	___	___
5	___	___	___	___	___
6	___	___	___	___	___
7	___	___	___	___	___
8	___	___	___	___	___
9	___	___	___	___	___
10	___	___	___	___	___
11	___	___	___	___	___
12	___	___	___	___	___
Medians	___	___	___	___	___

Muller-Lyer

Table 4.2. *Median data from 10 subjects for 5 angles of arrowhead.*

Subject	\multicolumn{5}{c}{Degree of Angle from Vertical}
	0	15	30	45	60
1	___	___	___	___	___
2	___	___	___	___	___
3	___	___	___	___	___
4	___	___	___	___	___
5	___	___	___	___	___
6	___	___	___	___	___
7	___	___	___	___	___
8	___	___	___	___	___
9	___	___	___	___	___
You	___	___	___	___	___
Means	___	___	___	___	___

You should now look very carefully at your data in Table 4.1. As explained in the Design section, these data represent a direct measure of the strength of the illusion, being the differences between the length of the Out and of the In Arrows at the point where you judged them to be equal. In fact they are the Out Arrow length minus the In Arrow length divided by two, which is in effect a percentage (the % difference between the perceived lengths of Out and In Arrows). A positive value indicates that the Out Arrow is perceived as longer than the In Arrow. How consistent were you in your judgment? Now look at the group data in Table 4.2. How does your data compare with the other subjects. In order to make any effect clearer, take the group means for each of the five angles of arrow and plot these in the form of a *bar graph* in Fig. 4.4.

Fig. 4.4. *Relationship between Arrowhead angle and strength of illusion.*

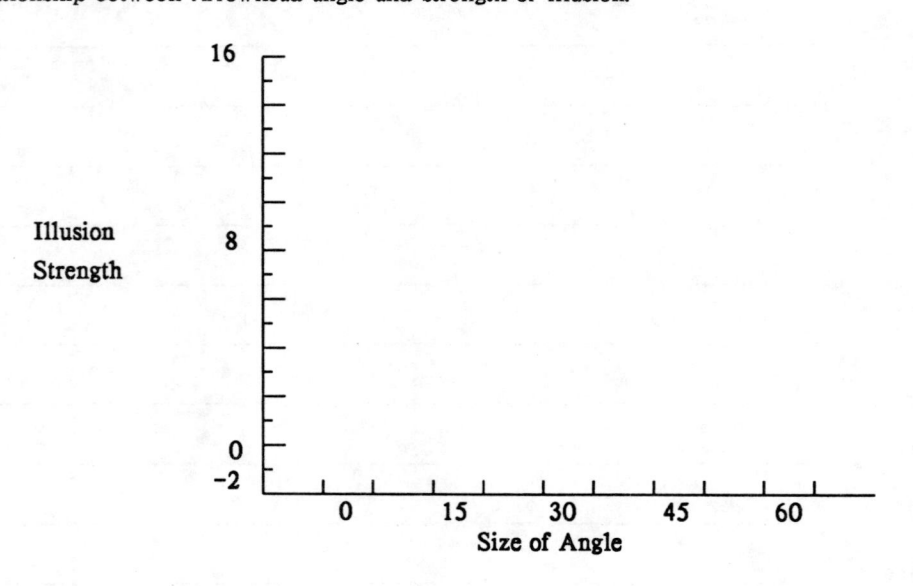

What evidence is there for an effect of the angle of the arrowhead lines on the size of the Muller-Lyer illusion effect and how else might you have shown this effect on a graph?

We could have analysed the strength of any effect of angle on the illusion by using a statistical test such as *Analysis of Variance* (ANOVA). However, this is a complex computational procedure and it would also be possible to use a series of *t-tests* to compare the group data for each of the possible pairs of angle. You may like to attempt this at a later date when you have had the opportunity to carry out a *matched-pairs t-test* (*t-test for correlated data*) in later chapters.

Discussion

In experiments of this type, it is usual to find that there is an effect of line angle such that the illusion decreases as the angle increases in extent. Why should this happen and does it help to explain why the Muller-Lyer illusion works at all? There are at least two reasons why one might expect this kind of result. The first arises from the possibility that the perceiver is not judging the correct lines when he makes his decision. If you look at Fig. 4.5 you will see that it is possible to draw a whole set of lines which link the three arrowheads together and it may be that the perceiver is taking an average of all the possible connecting lines. Obviously, the smaller the angle of the arrowhead, the greater the difference between the averages of the lines and therefore the stronger the illusion effect.

Fig. 4.5. *Example of Muller-Lyer figures with imaginary connecting lines.*

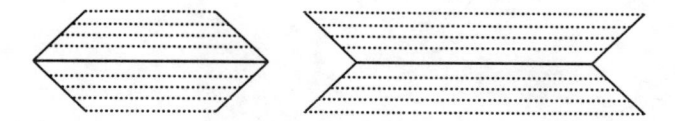

Another possible explanation has been made in terms of optical blur. This refers to the eye's occasional inability to provide a sharp discrimination between two points or lines that are closely adjacent. The effect of this is for the brain to interpret two points as forming one single point at a different location in space. This can be seen in Fig. 4.6.

Fig. 4.6 *The effect of image blur on two adjacent points that are a) close and b) very close.*

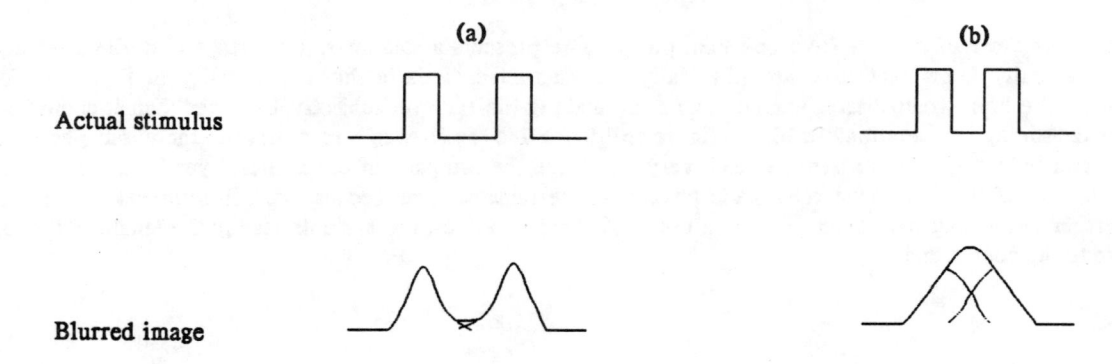

The effect of this image blur on the Muller-Lyer figure is demonstrated in Fig. 4.7 in which it can be seen that the Arrow In line is made to appear shorter, while the Arrow Out line appears longer.

Muller-Lyer

Fig. 4.7. *The effect of image blur on the Muller-Lyer figure.*

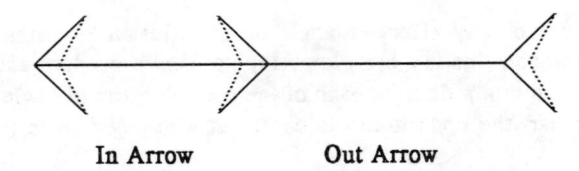

In Arrow   Out Arrow

It is possible to set up an experimental situation which allows us to distinguish between these alternative explanations. If we make our Muller-Lyer figures out of dots rather than lines (see Fig. 4.8), it should still be possible to average imaginary lines between the dots, but the effect of image blur should be very much reduced or eliminated. Therefore we would expect to find a significant illusion effect if the "Averaging" explanation is valid, but not if the "Image Blur" explanation is more appropriate. Of course, we would have to think of some way to prevent the subject simply counting the dots to equalize the line length. Can you suggest any way of doing this?

Fig. 4.8. *Example of the Muller-Lyer figure constructed from dots.*

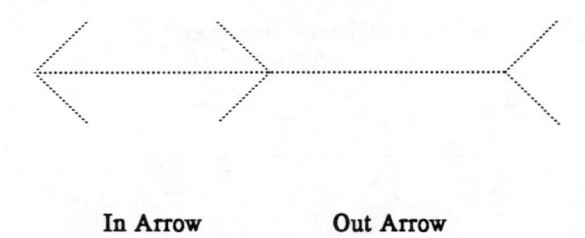

In Arrow   Out Arrow

However, while the Averaging and Image Blur explanations are quite interesting, there are other interpretations of the illusion effect. Amongst these, perhaps the most interesting is that put forward by Gregory (1966) who believes that the Muller-Lyer and other illusion effects are the direct result of our experience with the world and of our tendency to perceive two-dimensional figures as three-dimensional, i.e. we make interpretations about any available depth information. Gregory has indeed shown that Muller-Lyer figures that are constructed from luminous wire are clearly seen as three-dimensional objects when viewed in the dark. How does this actually explain the illusion effect though? One extra factor has to be added, that of *size constancy*.

If we look at the floor of a room from one end, the far side presents a smaller retinal image than the near side although we actually know that they are physically the same size. This is shown pictorially in Fig. 4.9. For example in a), the brain compensates to some extent by making the far side subjectively larger than it should be. This is size constancy in operation. In b), the figure still looks like the floor of a room despite the missing sections of the edge and indeed the figure begins to look very much like the two parts of the Muller-Lyer figure. In c), the far and near sides of the floor have been made physically the same size, but because we still interpret the top line as being further away than the bottom line, as a result of the depth cues, the brain scales-up the length of the top line relative to the bottom one.

Fig. 4.9. *The Muller-Lyer derived from our experience with the floors of rooms.*

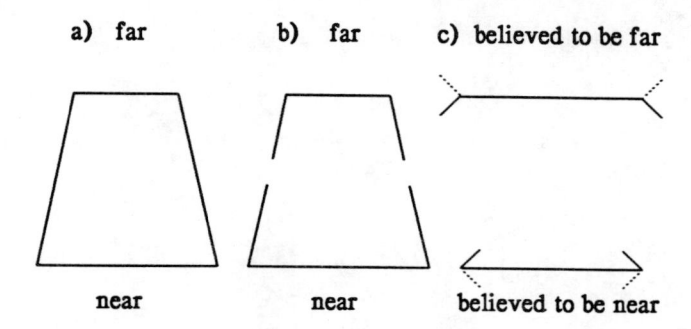

        a) far   b) far   c) believed to be far

        near   near   believed to be near

This interpretation, which is based on the perception of two-dimensional objects as three-dimensional ones and the operation of size constancy, can also be used to explain the Ponzo illusion. If you refer back to Fig. 4.1, you probably have no difficulty in imagining the Ponzo figure as a railway track. In this case the upper horizontal line should be further away than the lower one and will therefore be scaled-up by size constancy. The Zollner illusion can be explained in a similar way. As for the Poggendorff illusion, it can be interpreted in terms of a combination of perceived depth and *shape constancy*, since the illusion resembles an overturned chair, where the two lines (diagonally opposite chair legs) would never be interpreted as meeting. See Fig. 4.10.

Fig. 4.10. *The Poggendorff illusion in two forms.*

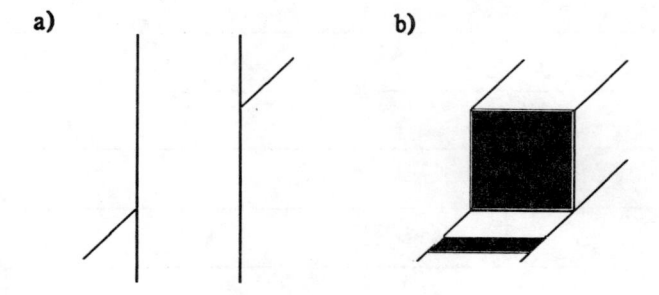

    a)   b)

Some evidence for this still controversial interpretation has been found in the investigation of other cultural groups whose environment is not rectilinear like that of Western cultures. For example, Deregowski (1972) has shown that Zulu tribesman, who live in a curvilinear environment of round walls and conical roofs, do not demonstrate any evidence of the Muller-Lyer illusion. This evidence can be criticized on the basis that the tribesman may not have really understood the task presented to them. Can you think of other problems that there might be with this kind of cross-cultural research?

However, some possible role for experience in illusion effects is at least partially confirmed by the finding that the strength of illusions like the Muller-Lyer reduces with increased exposure (Gillam, 1980).

Think about the alternative explanations for the Muller-Lyer illusion and consider how well they deal with the established facts. In particular, look at the various forms of the Muller-Lyer that are illustrated in Fig. 4.11 and note that it is possible to demonstrate a Muller-Lyer kind of effect using a tactile form of the figure with subjects who were born blind.

Muller-Lyer

Fig. 4.11. *Variations of the Muller-Lyer figure.*

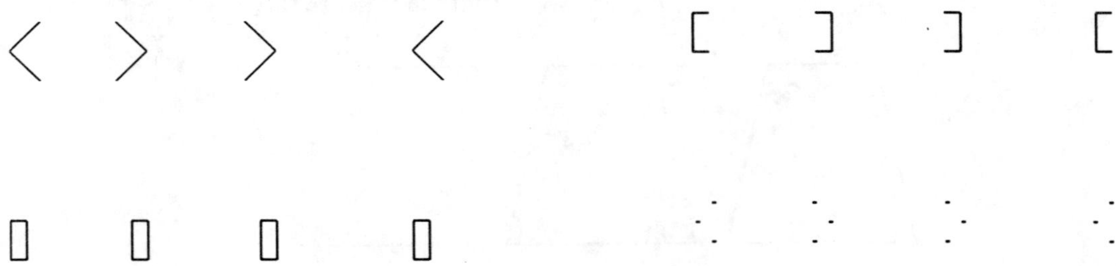

⟨ ⟩   ⟩   ⟨   [   ]   ]   [

▯ ▯ ▯ ▯   .   .   .   .
                .   .   .   .

What is your opinion about the best explanation for the Muller-Lyer? Is there a single best explanation? You may like to use this space to summarize your own conclusions.

_____
_____
_____
_____
_____
_____
_____
_____
_____
_____
_____
_____
_____

Recommended Reading
Gregory, R.L. (1966). *Eye and Brain*. London: Weidenfeld & Nicolson. (Chapter 9).

References
Coren, S., and Girgus, J.S. (1978). *Seeing is Deceiving: The Psychology of Visual Illusions*. Hillsdale N.J.: Erlbaum.
Day, R.H. (1980). Visual Illusions. In M.A. Jeeves (Ed.), *Psychology Survey, No. 3*. London: Allen & Unwin.
Deregowski, J.B. (1972). Pictorial perception and culture. *Scientific American, 227*, 82-88.
Gillam, B. (1980). Geometrical illusions. *Scientific American, 242*, 102-111.
Robinson, J.O. (1972). *The Psychology of Visual Illusions*. London: Hutchinson.

Notes

Notes

Chapter 5: Prisoner's Dilemma

As there is very little point in running this experiment once you have read the background to it, it is imperative that you read the instructions below and then run yourself as a subject in the experiment before reading the remainder of the text.

Instructions to Subjects

There are two participants in this task, one participant is yourself while the second participant is known as the "other" and will in this case be the computer though it could well have been another person. On the screen you will see a matrix like that of Table 6.1. The task consists of a number of trials. On every trial each participant has to make a choice, one choice is "red" the other is "black". You make your choice by pressing the key corresponding to the first letter of your choice. After you have made your choice on a trial, that choice will be shown on the screen. Thus if you press the R key, the screen indicates your action by flashing your "Red" indicator in the matrix. Similarly, if you press B, that fact will be illustrated in the same manner. The other has to make a choice simultaneously with your choosing. The other's choices are shown in the same way as yours. On each trial, both participants have to make a choice, so you will appreciate that one of your own and one of the other's choice indicators will flash.

Table 6.1. *The pay-off matrix for the present experiment.*

Your Total

		OTHER Red		OTHER Black	
SELF	Red	3	3	-10	10
	Black	10	-10	-5	-5

Associated with each combination of your choice with the other's choice, are what are known as *pay-offs*. Thus in each of the four cells of the matrix there are two numbers. The number on the left in each cell is your pay-off. That is, it represents the number of points to be added to your total score if that cell is chosen by both participants. Similarly, the number on the right in each cell is the other's pay-off. When both participants have made their choices then, and only then, do their choice indicators flash and both pay-offs in the matrix flash also. If you pressed the red key and the other chose red, then you would get 3 points. If you pressed the red key and the other chose black, then you would lose 10 points and the other would get 10 points. If you pressed the black key and the other chose red, then you would get 10 points and the other would lose 10 points. If you pressed the black key and the other chose black, then you would lose 5 points and the other would lose 5 points. At the end of each trial your total score will be updated.

During each trial you will get some time to make up your mind and then you will be asked to press the RETURN key when you are ready to choose. Soon after you have indicated that you are ready, the word PRESS will appear on the screen. When you see PRESS you should then press the key of your choice. When both participants have chosen, the relevant matrix entries will flash and the score will be updated.

There will be a number of trials. You will be told when to stop. All the trials will be played with the same other and using the above pay-off matrix. Your aim in the course of the trials, is to make as many points for yourself as possible without either trying to make more points than the other or trying to defeat the other. The other has exactly the same goal - to make as many points as possible for itself without trying to gain more points than you and without trying to defeat you. When you actually make your choice, the other will have no knowledge of which key you pressed till it has made its own choice, at which time both choices will appear on the screen simultaneously. At the time of choice the other has exactly the same knowledge as you - it will not "cheat" by waiting till you choose before deciding on its own choice.

DO NOT TURN THE PAGE OR READ ANY MORE AT THIS POINT. CARRY ON AND RUN THE EXPERIMENT.

Prisoner's Dilemma

Results

Now that the experiment is over, copy the results given to you by the computer into Tables 5.2 and 5.3.

Table 5.2. *Results of the Prisoner's Dilemma Game.*

Trial	Choice	SELF Points	Total	Trial	Choice	OTHER Points	Total
1				1			
2				2			
3				3			
4				4			
5				5			
6				6			
7				7			
8				8			
9				9			
10				10			
11				11			
12				12			
13				13			
14				14			
15				15			
16				16			
17				17			
18				18			
19				19			
20				20			

Table 5.3. *Summary of the results of 12 subjects on the Prisoner's Dilemma game.*

Subject	Number of Cooperative moves
1	_____
2	_____
3	_____
4	_____
5	_____
6	_____
7	_____
8	_____
9	_____
10	_____
11	_____
You	_____
Group Mean	_____

Introduction to Experimental Gaming

Social psychology has not always been considered an exact experimental science and it has been criticized for being very subjective and for having only a narrow range of applicability. However, much recent social psychology research has been very experimental and this is particularly obvious in the area of study known as experimental gaming research. This involves the analysis of the way that people interact with one another when they are in game-playing situations. The primary interest of the social psychologist is not in how people actually play games, but in what games can tell us about how people interact with each other in real life, using strategies such as cooperation and exploitation. Games are simply being used as models of real life, although whether they are adequate models remains a matter of some debate.

Most gaming research has made use of very simple games which involve only a limited range of possible behaviours on the part of subjects. Typically, the experimenter will provide varying amounts of incentive for cooperation and for competition between two players. These players will probably never meet and will be extremely limited in the amount of communication that they are allowed with each other. The point of such experiments is to establish the minimal conditions required to obtain conflict or cooperation between two individuals, in a situation in which preconceptions and prior attitudes are hopefully excluded because the game is completely novel.

One of the first such games was devised originally by Deutsch and Krauss (1960; 1962) and constituted a trucking game in which two subjects were asked to play the role of the owner of their own haulage firm. Each player was told that he would be given a fixed reward for delivering a load to a specific destination, and was warned that there

Prisoner's Dilemma

would be a deduction from this depending on the time taken for the delivery. There were only two possible routes for each truck (see Fig. 5.1.), a long way which ensured that the time penalties would be greater than the reward and a shorter way along a section of one-track road. If this route was taken the reward would be greater than the penalty, but only one truck could take the road at a time because the two trucks had to travel in opposite directions. As a result, the players could only maximize their rewards by cooperating and taking the one-way route on alternate runs.

Fig. 5.1 *Possible routes in the Trucking game.*

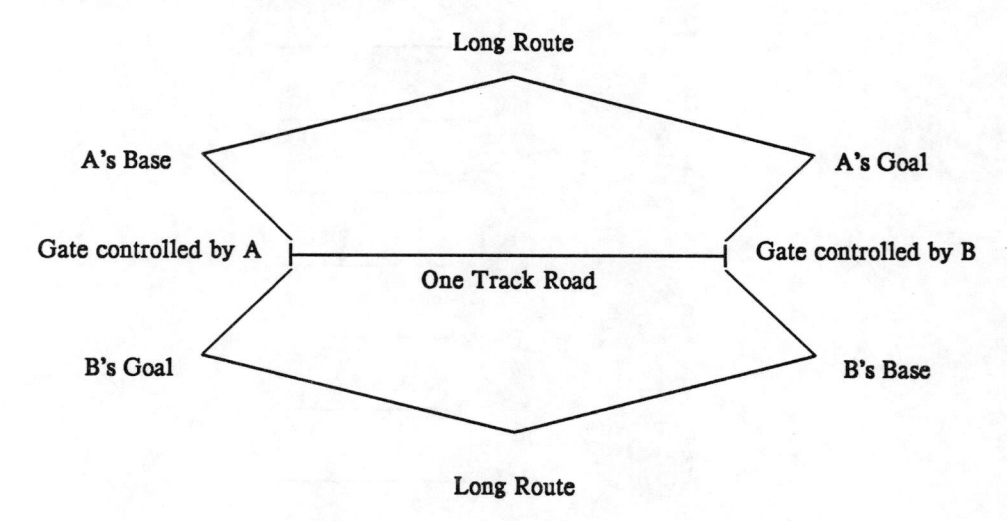

```
                        Long Route
                     _____
                    /              \
          A's Base /                \ A's Goal
                  <                  >
Gate controlled by A |――――――――――――――| Gate controlled by B
                     | One Track Road|
                  <                  >
          B's Goal \                / B's Base
                    _____/
                        Long Route
```

Surprisingly, frequent conflict and competition is found in this game rather than the apparently more sensible alternative of cooperation. A number of factors were found to influence the extent of cooperation and a particularly important factor was found to be the presence of threat. A variation of the original game was developed in which gates were introduced at either end of the one-track road. Each player controlled the gate at his own entrance to the road and the degree of competition increased enormously under these conditions, a fact which Deutsch (1969) attempted to apply directly to international conflict.

The Prisoner's Dilemma Game

Perhaps the best known of all experimental games, however, is the *Prisoner's Dilemma* game, or PD for short and it is this game which you should have already played on the computer and which will now be discussed. The PD game originated as an imaginary situation involving two criminals. Both had been arrested for committing a serious crime and were being held in separate cells. Unfortunately there was no definite evidence against either criminal and the prosecutor was hoping that one or both would confess. The prosecutor explained the situation separately to each criminal as follows:

> *You have only two alternatives, you can either confess or not confess. If neither of you confesses, I shall trump up some minor charge and you will both be jailed for a short sentence. If you both confess then you will be found guilty, but I will recommend a sentence that is lighter than the maximum. However, if only one of you confesses, then the confessor will be set free because of turning Queen's evidence, whereas the other criminal will receive a maximum sentence.*

Another way to conceptualize this situation is to produce a pay-off matrix which clearly sets out the outcomes of the different possibilities. This has been done in Table 5.4.

Table 5.4. *A pay-off matrix for the Prisoner's Dilemma game.*

		Prisoner B Confess	Prisoner B Not Confess
Prisoner A	Confess	6 years for A 6 years for B	A goes free 12 years for B
	Not Confess	12 years for A B goes free	1 year for A 1 year for B

When this type of pay-off matrix for situations is looked at, there can be seen to be two kinds of game that are possible – *zero-sum* and *non-zero-sum* games. In the zero-sum situation, one person cannot benefit without taking something from another, whereas in the non-zero-sum situation both persons can potentially benefit if they adopt the correct cooperative strategy. The PD game is a non-zero-sum game, sometimes also termed a *mixed-motive* game and it is this type of game which we have been examining in this chapter.

Design

This has really been more of a demonstration than an experiment and it is not easy to make the details fit the standard report format. However, what we have is a situation in which two players, in our case a subject and the computer, are allowed two possibilities of response in a fixed situation. These responses are to cooperate (both choose Red) or to compete (one or both chooses Black). What happens in terms of benefits to the players as a result of the response they make depends on what they do and what the other player does. In our case it depends on what the subject does and what the computer does. In fact the computer, after it makes its first move which is always a cooperative one, adopts the consistent strategy of making the choice that the subject made on the previous trial. Thus if the subject cooperates on Trial 1, then the computer will make a cooperative choice on Trial 2. If the subject does not cooperate on Trial 1, then the computer will not cooperate on Trial 2. This has been termed the "tit-for-tat" or TFT principle and it clearly acts to reward the subject for cooperating and to punish him for failing to cooperate. It has been shown to be amongst the best strategies for promoting cooperation.

The meaning of these responses in terms of the gains and losses concerned is shown in the matrix of outcomes (the pay-off matrix) for our experiment in Table 5.5.

Table 5.5. *The pay-off matrix for the present experiment.*

Your Total _____

		Computer (C) Red	Computer (C) Black
Subject (S)	Red	+3 for S +3 for C	−10 for S +10 for C
	Black	+10 for S −10 for C	−5 for S −5 for C

Prisoner's Dilemma

Subjects
You will have run yourself as a subject in this experiment and you will have been given data from 11 other subjects.

Stimuli
The stimuli consisted of a sequence of 20 presentations of a choice matrix, as in Table 5.1. On each presentation of the stimulus matrix, up-dated information about your total points score was displayed.

Procedure
The computer presented a set of instructions which were broadly the same as those provided in the Instructions to Subjects above.

Results
You will have been given a list of your own and the computer's responses and scores for each trial which you should have copied into Table 5.1. You will also have been given the cooperation scores for 11 subjects who have already run this experiment, which data you should have entered into Table 5.2. You should work out the number of co-operative moves you made and enter this at the end of Table 5.2. (Cooperative moves are those trials on which you picked RED).

Calculate the average number of cooperative moves for the group and express this as a percentage of the total number of cooperative moves that were possible. Your estimate is

_____%?

The maximum number of points that you could have accrued if you had been as cooperative as the other player was prepared to be was 60 points (3 on each of 20 trials). In fact if you had worked out the other's strategy and predicted the number of trials you could have scored 67 points by competing rather than cooperating on the last trial only.

How would you describe the other's play in the game? Did you realise that the other was seeking to be cooperative, but would punish you if you were competitive? Are you a cooperative individual or do you often find yourself competing with others? Are you happy about the validity of making this kind of generalization about people?

Discussion
The most important result gleaned from PD research, a result which has consistently been demonstrated, is that only infrequently is any degree of cooperation achieved. The average amount of cooperation in terms of the percentage of trials on which one or other side makes a cooperative move varies between 30% and 40% (about one in every three trials). How does your estimate of the amount of cooperation in this experiment compare with the usual results from the PD game?

As a consequence of this finding, the main interest of researchers has been to determine the factors which prevent cooperation developing in the PD game. One important factor that has been suggested is that many subjects appear to adopt a short-term strategy rather than a long-term one in their responding. This refers to the tendency to be concerned with an immediate profit or loss as opposed to a concern with the long-term effectiveness of ones actions. The short-term focus will not lead to cooperation while the long-term focus will. Short-term thinking is a consequence of failing to form any social expectations about the "other" in the game, paying little attention to the existence of the other and the possible influence that one may have upon the other. At the opposite extreme, adoption of the long-term strategy depends upon the subject believing that cooperation is the sensible solution, coupled with his expectation that the other will also want to cooperate (Pruitt and Kimmell, 1977).

It has been argued that there is a tendency for the PD game to promote short-term, trial-by-trial thinking because of certain artificial aspects of the PD game situation itself. Amongst these aspects are the reward structure of the game and the lack of communication between the players. If we examine the reward aspect first we can see that many researchers have criticized the PD game for being exactly that, "just a game", and they have argued that subjects will not play the game in any serious way because they are only playing for somewhat meaningless points, or at best for a few pence. If there are no real and worthwhile rewards to be gained, why should subjects cooperate at all? Certainly there are a number of studies which have shown that increasing the rewards in other games such as the Trucking game have the effect of increasing cooperation considerably (Gallo, 1966), but the PD game is essentially different from these other games. In the Trucking game, for example, the way to maximize the reward for both players is for them to take turns to win the maximum individual total on alternate trials. In the PD game, the maximum reward is obtained through one player beating the other, and thus mutual cooperation is achieved only by both players agreeing to give up the chance of the maximum pay-off for himself. The result of this is that increasing the rewards in the PD game not only makes it more beneficial for the individual to cooperate, but it also makes it more profitable to compete. Such studies as have been carried out tend to agree that there is only a slight increase in cooperation as the rewards are increased in real value (Gallo and Sheposh, 1971). What has more influence on cooperation in the PD game is altering the relationship between the pay-off for competing and that for cooperating, for example, one can increase the pay-off for mutual cooperation and diminish the pay-off for competition. Such relative alterations to the pay-off matrix will have the effect of changing each subject's goals and his perception of the likely intentions of the other player.

The "lack of communication" factor is also an interesting one. It is of course a fundamental part of the original game and was intended to increase the level of uncertainty about the intentions of the other player and it has been continued often because of experimental necessity. After all, if the subject is playing against a computer, any form of interactive communication is going to be rather hard to achieve. Perhaps unsurprisingly, when players are allowed the opportunity for a communication session, perhaps at the midway point of the game, there is generally a subsequent increase in the amount of cooperation (Scodel, Minas, Ratoosh and Lipetz, 1959). However, it needs to be remembered that many players will exploit an opportunity for communication as an extension of their moves in the game and pass information that is designed to assist their overall competitive strategy rather than promote competition. A further interesting comment that has been made about preventing communication is that this has the effect of isolating the individual, making him more inward directed and less open to social norms of reciprocity and cooperation. Clear evidence for the importance of isolation in reducing cooperation comes from a study of Wichman (1970). When female students played the PD game in isolation from each other, the measured rate of cooperation was 41%. When they could see but not hear each other this rose to 48%. When they could hear but not see each other the rate of cooperation was 72% and when they could both see and hear each other it was 87%. The more natural the communication, the greater the cooperation, perhaps because of the adoption of the long-term perspective.

One final point of interest refers to the previously acknowledged fact that each player makes some kind of interpretation of the goals and intentions of the other player. It is only when this interpretation is of a desire for cooperation that the adoption of a long-term perspective will be effective in promoting cooperation. The problem is that people tend to base their interpretations of another's intentions upon their own. Thus the person who is essentially cooperatively directed will perceive the actions of others as being cooperative while the competitive spirit will make the opposite deduction about the same set of actions. Perhaps the greatest scope for this subjectivity in interpretation lies in the situation where the game partner chooses the competitive response (in our case Black). It could be that this choice is actually exploitive, but it could also be taken to be a defensive response where the partner is held to have felt that the subject was also about to choose the Black response (Kelley and Stahelski, 1970). This confusion about intentions is in fact more likely to occur in the PD game than in many others and considerable debate about the operation of *attributions* in the PD game has been presented in the literature (Miller and Holmes, 1975), particularly as regards the "self-fulfilling prophecy" of the competitively oriented player.

You may recall that the introduction to experimental gaming research put forward the argument that games could provide valid models for real-life situations and one might like to ask how successfully the results of games like the PD game have been applied. Many researchers have in fact been very wary about directly applying their laboratory results, although a few have been less reticent. For example, Deutsch (1969, 1973) has attempted to explain quite broad social issues in terms of gaming models. At the present moment it is probably too early to say with any certainty to what extent such attempts can be considered to be successful. The a priori assumption is being made that laboratory principles can be extrapolated to real-life situations, but there have been no clear empirical demonstrations that this kind of assumption is justified (Campbell, 1957). Pruitt and Kimmell (1977) argue that the very artificiality of the laboratory setting for research forces individuals into behaving in an atypical way that does not reflect their learned, habitual ways of responding. If this is the case, then it is sensible to maintain a degree of caution with regard to experimental gaming research.

Recommended Reading
Eiser, J.R. (1980). *Cognitive Social Psychology*. London: McGraw Hill. (Chapter 7).

References
Bixenstein, V.E., and Gaebelein, J.W. (1971). Strategies of "real" opponents in eliciting cooperative choice in a Prisoner's Dilemma game. *Journal of Conflict Resolution, 15,* 157-166.

Campbell, D.T. (1957). Factors relevant to the validity of experiments in social settings. *Psychological Bulletin, 54,* 297-312.

Deutsch, M. (1960), The effect of motivational orientation upon trust and suspicion. *Human Relations, 13,* 122-139.

Deutsch, M. (1969). Socially relevant science: Reflections on some studies of interpersonal conflict. *American Psychologist, 24,* 1076-1092.

Deutsch, M. (1973). *The Resolution of Conflict: Constructive and Destructive Processes.* New Haven: Yale University.

Deutsch, M., and Krauss, R.M. (1960). The effect of threat on interpersonal bargaining. *Journal of Abnormal and Social Psychology, 61,* 181-189.

Deutsch, M., and Krauss, R.M. (1962). Studies of interpersonal bargaining. *Journal of Conflict Resolution, 6,* 52-76.

Gallo, P.S. (1966). Prisoner's of our own dilemma? In L.S. Wrightsman, J. O'Conner and N.J. Baker (Eds.), *Cooperation and Competition: Readings on Mixed-motive Games.* Belmont: Wadsworth.

Gallo, P.S., and Sheposh, J. (1971). Effects of incentive magnitude on cooperation in the Prisoner's Dilemma game: A reply to Gumpert, Deutsch and Epstein. *Journal of Personality, 19,* 42-46.

Hofstader, D.R. (1983). Metamagical themas: computer tournaments of the Prisoner's Dilemma suggest how cooperation evolves. *Scientific American, 248 (5),* 14-20.

Hofstader, D.R. (1983). Metamagical themas: the calculus of cooperation is tested through a lottery. *Scientific American, 248 (6),* 14-18.

Kelley, H.H., and Stahelski, A.J. (1970). Errors in perception of intentions in a mixed-motive game. *Journal of Experimental Social Psychology, 6,* 379-400.

Mills, J. (1969). *Experimental Social Psychology.* London: MacMillan.

Miller, D.T., and Holmes, J.G. (1975). The role of situational restrictiveness on self-fulfilling prophecies. A theoretical and empirical extension of Kelley and Stahelski's Triangle Hypothesis. *Journal of Personality and Social Psychology, 31,* 661-673.

Pruitt, D.G., and Kimmel, M.J. (1977). Twenty years of experimental gaming: critique, synthesis, and suggestions for the future. *Annual Review of Psychology, 28,* 363-392.

Sampson, E.E. (1971). *Social Psychology and Contemporary Society.* New York: Wiley.

Scodel, A., Minas, J.S., Ratoosh, P., and Lipetz, M. (1959). Some descriptive aspects of two-person non-zero-sum games, I. *Journal of Conflict Resolution, 3,* 114-119.

Wichman, H. (1970). Effects of isolation and communication on cooperation in a two-person game. *Journal of Personality and Social Psychology, 16,* 114-120.

Notes

Notes

Chapter 6: Extra-sensory Perception (ESP)

There is a field of psychology which has never been completely acceptable to the profession, but which has been steadily growing in stature through recent years. This is the field of *parapsychology*, a name which covers research into psychic phenomena such as *telepathy*, *clairvoyance*, *precognition* and *psychokinesis*. While it is still true that the majority of psychologists are very sceptical about the claims of most psychical researchers, it is now at least realised that research into psychic phenomena represents a major testing-ground for the methods of experimental psychology. Thus it has been argued that the scientific method of controlled experimentation can be applied to the paranormal and that this application will not simply provide valuable evidence about the possible existence of paranormal phenomena, but will also test the scientific rigour of our research methods and analytical techniques.

The phenomena which have received most study are those subsumed under the label of extra-sensory perception or ESP, where information is held to be obtained at a distance and not through the normal sensory mechanisms. Information obtained about people comes through *telepathy* and information about objects or events comes through *clairvoyance*. There are many reports of these phenomena in popular literature as well as in scientific journals, but most if not all have the drawback that they are inadequately documented, the events are not independently witnessed and supported and they are by their very nature not repeatable. What is required is to bring ESP research into the laboratory where events can be carefully controlled and multiple replications can be carried out of any given procedure in order to establish the reliability of the results obtained.

The first important attempt to develop a standard laboratory technique for assessing ESP was made by Rhine in the 1930's when he suggested that subjects be asked to guess the sequence in which cards would be drawn from a deck of 5 cards (see Fig. 6.1).

Fig. 6.1. *A form of Rhine's 5 ESP cards.*

It was considered that the ability to *perform better than chance* in successfully guessing the cards drawn would be a good way to measure ESP ability and it should be possible to exclude the possibility of any information being obtained through the conventional senses or of any biases or errors occurring in the recording of the guesses that are made.

That this experimental method could have been developed, depended upon prior developments in statistical theory in order to establish scientifically, exactly what is meant by the commonly used expression *better than chance*. If on a given trial, a subject were to guess which card had been drawn from a deck of 5 different and randomly sorted cards, he would have a 1 in 5 chance of being correct (this may be restated as there being a probability of being correct of 0.2). So if 5 guesses were made, we would expect 1 correct guess out of the 5. However, if that subject made several thousand sets of 5 guesses, then on a few occasions the subject will get 5 correct, on more occasions he will get 4 correct and so on, with the majority of occasions resulting in only 1 correct guess. In other words, the results obtained would demonstrate scatter or variability around the average and as with so many measures or scores that scatter can be described mathematically and indeed can be demonstrated graphically by the *normal curve*.

The mathematical situation presented by the card guessing task is known as a binomial one since there are only two classes of guess, "right" and "wrong". The probability (Y) that any given number of guesses (X) will be correct by chance given a particular number of selections (N) is calculated from the formula:

$$Y = \frac{N!}{X!(N-X)!} \times p^X \times q^{(N-X)}$$

ESP

In this formula, *N!* means *N* factorial and *p* stands for the probability of a correct guess on a trial. In our card drawing task this means that p would equal 0.2; q stands for the probability of being wrong, which in our example would be 1 − p, i.e. 0.8. If we take every value of X between 0 and 100 and calculate the probability of obtaining that number of guesses correct in 100 trials, then the results can be graphed. Put more mathematically, for N = 100 the distribution of X from 1 to N is shown in Fig. 6.2 where it can be seen that the average score is 20 correct out of 100 guesses and that scoring very low (making lots of errors) is as hard as scoring very high (making lots of accurate guesses). In fact, it is not even possible to show the probability of scoring less than 7 or more than 35 guesses correct on the graph because the probabilities are as low as 0.0002.

Fig. 6.2. *Probability of guessing ESP cards correctly by chance in 100 trials.*

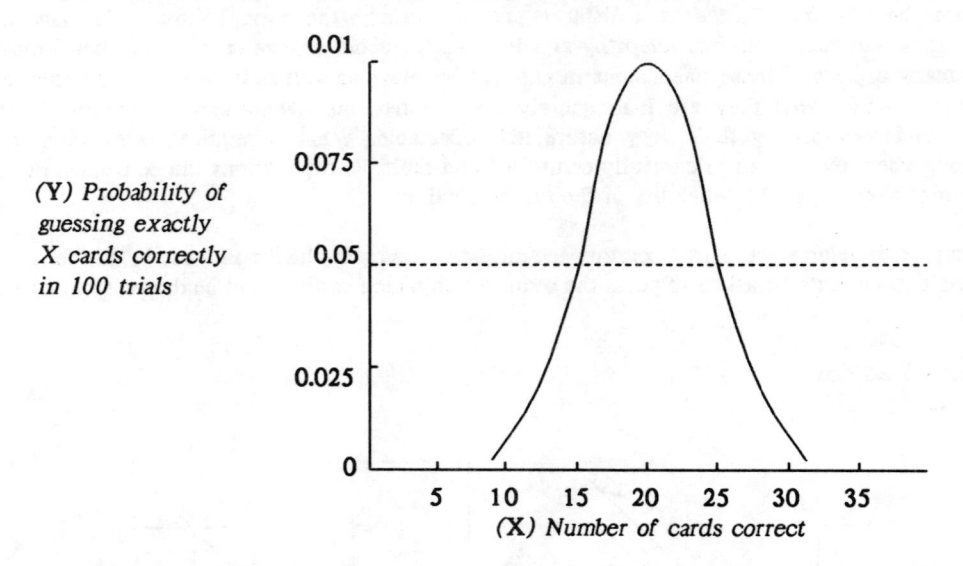

In most psychology experiments we are prepared to accept that an event is not random, that is, does not occur by chance, if its probability of occurrence by chance is less than 5 in 100. To restate this, we would accept the validity of an event with a probability of p<0.05. We can therefore read from the graph those values of X which would represent a probability of less than 5 in 100 by projecting down from the normal curve at those points where it intersects the probability value 0.05 shown by the dotted line. These values are approximately 15 and 25. You will have noticed perhaps that the assumption that is being made statistically, is that very low scores are as significant in their departure from the mean as are very high scores. Indeed, so-called "negative ESP" has been reported in the literature where subjects consistently do less well in testing than we would expect by chance.

In fact, in ESP research, the actual test of the operation of some non-chance factor in a guessing sequence is usually derived from the standard deviation:

$$(N \times p \times q)^{0.5}$$

This represents the amount of variability or scatter in the data around the mean value itself, the mean being $N \times p$. The actual metric used to assess ESP is called the *critical ratio* (CR) and this is derived from the following formula:

$$CR = \frac{X - pN}{(N \times p \times q)^{0.5}}$$

If the CR is zero, then one can be certain that chance alone has been influencing results, but it has been accepted amongst many ESP researchers that if the CR is greater than 2.7 then there is the possibility of a non-chance effect that may be ESP. A CR of 2.7 has a probability of occurring by chance of p = 0.0035. We will also adopt this strict criterion.

Design
This is a single-subject experiment in which you the subject will make a series of guesses about the card which has just been selected at random by the computer. The *independent variable* is therefore the type of symbol on the card, and the *dependent variable* is the accuracy of the guesses made.

Stimuli
The stimuli are the numbers 1 to 5, and are thus numeric versions of the cards originally developed by Rhine. There are therefore 5 cards in all and the computer will select at random from this set on 100 occasions.

Procedure
You will sit at the computer which will make a selection from the number set 1, 2, 3, 4 and 5. On each trial, when it has selected a number, it will give the message "Computer's selection complete". You will then be asked to make your own guess about the number that the computer has just selected. You do this by pressing the computer key corresponding to your chosen number between 1 and 5. Once you have done this, the computer will reveal its selection. When you are ready to begin the next trial, you will press the large SPACE BAR. There will be one practice trial.

You should try to place yourself in a quiet, calm state so that any ESP abilities that you have are allowed the maximum opportunity to express themselves. Remember, many people who did not believe they had any abilities have found themselves to be very good at this type of task. You may be another! Try not to take too long to make your choice, but remember to take a break for a few minutes at any point that you are feeling tired and cannot concentrate. There is no point in doing any of the experiment if you are not really trying your best! Of course we do not really know if trying, or being calm, or being in any particular state actually influences psychic ability, this is simply a guess about the way in which it might work.

You should record the sequence of your guesses and of the correct selections made by the computer on the Record Sheet at the end of this chapter.

Results
After you have completed the 100 trials, the computer will tell you how many of the numbers you guessed correctly and how many you got wrong. It will also tell you what your CR (critical ratio) is. Remember that a CR equal to or greater than 2.7 represents that value at which we can entertain the possibility of ESP being at work! Write your number of correct guesses and CR in Table 6.1.

Table 6.1. *Results on an ESP card guessing task for a single subject.*

Number of Guesses Correct	Critical Ratio
_____	_____

Discussion
There have been two large-scale experiments, of a broadly similar kind to this one, which were carried out on the radio. In America, Goodfellow (1938) reported the results of a study sponsored by the Zenith Radio Corporation which asked the listeners to a particular series of programmes to guess which cards were being telepathically communicated by a group of "senders". The BBC have carried out a similar study where listeners were to guess a sequence of playing cards that had been set out in the studio. In neither case was there any evidence that the sample who replied were demonstrating better than chance responding. However, what was particularly interesting

was that there was a great deal of consistency in the patterns or sequences which were most commonly reported. This consistency was traced to two factors:
1) the influence of subtle and often unintentional suggestions in the instructions read out to the listeners
2) the enduring dispositions or set demonstrated by the listeners.

The first point raises the critical methodological issue that subjects are in a situation where they wish to do well, and particularly to do what the experimenter wishes them to do. They are therefore sensitive to every little bit of information that is potentially available to them and can be readily swayed in a particular direction of responding by very subtle hints and cues. This is one reason why the preparation of Instructions to Subjects is a far more important activity in research than is usually understood. It is also the reason why it is usually better (if often somewhat impractical) for the experimenter conducting any experiment not to know what the actual purpose of the experiment is or at least not to know the experimental group to which the subject belongs. This "Experimenter Bias" effect has been studied in some detail by Rosenthal (1963). In one study he told a group of experimenters that the rats they were to test had been especially bred for their intelligence, while he told a second group that their rats were particularly dull. Naturally there were no real differences between the groups of rats, but the expectancies of the experimenters still led to them finding better results for the supposedly "bright" rats than for the "dim" rats. This type of effect has been repeated over-and-over again with human subjects by other experimenters and it has been noted that the Experimenter Bias effect is not simply the result of cheating but often involves very subtle, non-verbal communication to the subjects and supporting this suggestion is the fact that this effect is much stronger when the subject can see the experimenter than when he can only hear him. One might ask how a group of rats could be influenced by the experimenter, but in fact it has been shown that the way experimenters handle the experimental animals can markedly influence their behaviour during testing. Of course, in our experimental situation there was no experimenter present, the computer took his place, but there were instructions which hopefully were sufficiently well designed to obviate bias.

The second point can be readily demonstrated by asking people to write down the sequence of results that they might imagine would occur from tossing a coin twenty times. What is typically found is that people will severely underestimate the number of sequential heads or tails that would be expected by chance. Thus, few instances of three or more heads will be reported, far fewer than should be expected to occur. It can be concluded from this that we have all developed our own crude estimates of chance (subjective probability), estimates which are not necessarily particularly accurate, but which we often use to make important decisions. (This opens up a very interesting area of psychological study -choice, decision-making and risk. See for example, Edwards and Tversky, 1967). If you think back to your own guesses, or better still, if you have recorded them, you may be able to spot certain sequences of numbers that are more common than others, and indeed if you think back to the experiment itself, you may remember actually thinking "I won't put a 2 for this trial because I just wrote a 2 down for the last trial".

By looking at your Record Sheet, it may also be possible for you to see if there are any delayed ESP effects in your results. Sometimes, researchers have reported subjects whose results on this type of card guessing task show no ESP effects until the guesses are related to the trial ahead or perhaps several trials ahead. Perhaps you are able to influence the computer's selection of numbers!

What were your results? Are you a good candidate for introduction to the Society for Psychical Research? Some subjects obtain CR's as large as 20 or more. If your results were markedly better than you would have expected by chance, e.g. a CR of 4 or 5, would you be confident that you really were demonstrating ESP? Consider this possibility instead. You are one person doing this experiment which has already been carried out by at least a thousand other subjects. What if every other subject failed to obtain significant results, would you not then have to consider your results in terms of all the subjects that had ever carried out this study? If you do this then you would reasonably expect your particular set of results to by found by a few subjects purely by chance. This is a major criticism of most experimental research, not just of ESP research, and it is particularly worrying because it is generally only positive results which are published in learned journals. The studies which have found negative results are usually never reported in print. Of course it has been argued that only a few people are able to demonstrate ESP and therefore that the results of the majority of subjects tested are irrelevant and that what we need to do is identify the unusual respondent and concentrate on repeated testing of them to establish the reliability and validity of their responding.

One final point that this suggestion of large individual differences in ESP introduces, is the possible relationship between ESP and certain other individual differences such as personality type. Sargent (1981) has reported that extroverted people score higher in ESP tests than do introverts and that people who are low in neuroticism score better than those who are high. If you have completed an Eysenck Personality Inventory, you may like to consider your ratings on these factors in relation to your scores in the present experiment. It has also been suggested that young children have more ESP ability than do adults, but no relationship has been found with measured intelligence.

Recommended Reading
Roediger, H.L., Rushton, J.P., Capaldi, E.D., and Paris, S.G. (1984). *Psychology*. Boston: Little, Brown. (Pages 118-119).

References
Beloff, J. (Ed.). (1974). *New Directions in Parapsychology*. London: Paul Elek.

Edwards, W., and Tversky, A. (1966). *Decision-making*. London: Penguin.

Eysenck, H.J., and Sargent, C. (1982). *Explaining the Unexplained*. London: Weidenfeld & Nicolson.

Goodfellow, L.D.A. (1938). A psychological interpretation of the results of the Zenith radio experiments in telepathy. *Journal of Experimental Psychology*, 23, 601-632.

Hyman, R. (1976). (1940). Uri Geller at SRI. *The Humanist*, May/June.

Rhine, J.B. *Extra-sensory Perception After Sixty Years*. New York: Holt.

Rhine, L.E. (1966). *ESP in Life and Lab*, New York: MacMillan.

Rosenthal, R. (1963). On the social psychology of the psychological experiment: the experimenter's hypothesis as unintended determinant of experimental results. *American Scientist*, 1963, 51, 268-283.

Society for Psychical Research. 1 Adam and Eve Mews, London W8.

Wolman, B.B.(Ed.). (1977). *Handbook of Parapsychology*, New York: Van Nostrand Reinfold.

ESP

Record Sheet

Trial	Computer	You	Trial	Computer	You	Trial	Computer	You
1	_____	_____	28	_____	_____	55	_____	_____
2	_____	_____	29	_____	_____	56	_____	_____
3	_____	_____	30	_____	_____	57	_____	_____
4	_____	_____	31	_____	_____	58	_____	_____
5	_____	_____	32	_____	_____	59	_____	_____
6	_____	_____	33	_____	_____	60	_____	_____
7	_____	_____	34	_____	_____	61	_____	_____
8	_____	_____	35	_____	_____	62	_____	_____
9	_____	_____	36	_____	_____	63	_____	_____
10	_____	_____	37	_____	_____	64	_____	_____
11	_____	_____	38	_____	_____	65	_____	_____
12	_____	_____	39	_____	_____	66	_____	_____
13	_____	_____	40	_____	_____	67	_____	_____
14	_____	_____	41	_____	_____	68	_____	_____
15	_____	_____	42	_____	_____	69	_____	_____
16	_____	_____	43	_____	_____	70	_____	_____
17	_____	_____	44	_____	_____	71	_____	_____
18	_____	_____	45	_____	_____	72	_____	_____
19	_____	_____	46	_____	_____	73	_____	_____
20	_____	_____	47	_____	_____	74	_____	_____
21	_____	_____	48	_____	_____	75	_____	_____
22	_____	_____	49	_____	_____	76	_____	_____
23	_____	_____	50	_____	_____	77	_____	_____
24	_____	_____	51	_____	_____	78	_____	_____
25	_____	_____	52	_____	_____	79	_____	_____
26	_____	_____	53	_____	_____	80	_____	_____
27	_____	_____	54	_____	_____	81	_____	_____

ESP

82	___	___	89	___	___	95	___	___
83	___	___	90	___	___	96	___	___
84	___	___	91	___	___	97	___	___
85	___	___	92	___	___	98	___	___
86	___	___	93	___	___	99	___	___
87	___	___	94	___	___	100	___	___
88	___	___						

Notes

Chapter 7: Mental Imagery

Exactly how we represent visual and visuo-spatial information in our minds has been of interest to psychologists and philosophers for a considerable time. There is some reason to believe that the representation is somewhat like an internal picture, image or map which is *isomorphic* to the original stimulus or stimulus array. This type of enquiry has considerable practical relevance since many important and some less important activities involve the utilisation of visual representations, e.g. route finding, interior design, and jigsaw puzzle solving. The whole topic of memorization and recall is also closely linked to the notion of visual imagery, and Neisser (1982) provides some interesting accounts of the varying role of imagery in the memory feats of people with very special memories (See section VII of Neisser's book). In fact, it is held by many researchers that pictorial stimuli are better remembered than verbal stimuli (Paivio, 1971) and that when words are stored using visual imagery, subjects remember more than if they had used *rote rehearsal* (Schnorr and Atkinson, 1969). As Neisser (1982) points out, however, not all the great memorists appear to use visual imagery for verbal materials.

Experiment One

An important focus of enquiry into the topic of mental imagery has been the investigation into such questions as How much is visual imaging like visual perception and to what extent can we use visual images in place of the "original percepts?" Psychologists have attempted to answer these questions in a number of ways. For example, Peterson and Graham (1974) asked their subjects to imagine a specific object and then presented it to them. These subjects detected the presence of the object faster than a comparable group of subjects who did not first imagine the object, which suggested to the researchers that visual imaging and perception share similar mechanisms. In a further experiment, Peterson (1975) argued that imagery involves a reconstruction of direct perception and therefore that memory for visual patterns that were only imagined should be comparable to memory for patterns that had actually been perceived (showing the reliance of both systems on the same processing mechanisms) and this was what was found.

The first of two experiments in this unit is a replication of a simple study by Moyer (1973) in which the experimenter sought to discover whether subjects could form mental images that closely resemble actual perceptions (percepts) and inspect these mental images in order to make decisions.

Design

This will be a within subjects design in which all subjects will be tested with the same set of stimulus materials. The independent variable will be the difference in physical size between the objects to be compared, with two levels of similarity being used – small and large. The dependent variable will be the time it takes the subjects to make a decision about the relative size of a pair of objects, i.e. which is the larger of two objects. There will be 32 trials, 16 at each level of the independent variable.

Subjects

You will test yourself as a subject in this experiment and you will be provided with data from a further 14 subjects who have previously run themselves.

Stimuli

The stimuli will be pairs of words which will appear on the computer screen, one to the right of a central fixation spot and one to the left. The words will be the common names of various animals such as lion and centipede.

Procedure

The computer will begin by presenting the instructions to subjects, followed by four practice trials during which you will be given *feedback* about the accuracy of your judgments. Each trial will begin with a READY? enquiry from the computer. Once you are ready, press the SPACE BAR to let the computer know and, immediately afterwards, it will present a cross in the centre of the screen followed in a second by a pair of stimuli, one on the left and one on the right.

Hold your two forefingers (index fingers) so that the left forefinger rests lightly on the "Q" key and the right forefinger so that it rests on the "P" key. These keys are on the extreme left and extreme right of keyboard. As soon as you possibly can, press one of these keys to indicate your decision. Press the Q key if you decide that the test stimulus on the left is the larger of the two stimuli and press the P key if you decide that the stimulus on the right is the larger.

Mental Imagery

The computer will make a "buzzing" noise if you make a wrong decision and will emit a "beep-beep" sound if you are responding too slowly.

Results

After you have completed the experiment, the computer will present the results of a group of 14 subjects, followed by your own results as the 15th subject. The results will be in the form of median decision times (reaction times) in milliseconds (msecs). Please copy these data carefully into Table 7.1.

AT THIS POINT, DO NOT READ ANY MORE OF THIS UNIT. CARRY ON AND RUN THE EXPERIMENT IN CASE YOUR RESPONSES ARE INFLUENCED BY READING FURTHER.

Mental Imagery

Table 7.1. *Median decision times for a group of 15 subjects.*

Subject	Physical Difference Small	Large
1	_____	_____
2	_____	_____
3	_____	_____
4	_____	_____
5	_____	_____
6	_____	_____
7	_____	_____
8	_____	_____
9	_____	_____
10	_____	_____
11	_____	_____
12	_____	_____
13	_____	_____
14	_____	_____
You	_____	_____
Means	_____	_____

You should calculate the means for each of the two columns, i.e. a mean value for the median scores for the small and for the large conditions. You can now graph these means in the form of a *bar graph* in Fig. 7.1. The first part of each bar is drawn for you.

Mental Imagery

Fig. 7.1. *Bar graph of the effect of relative size difference of two objects on decision time.*

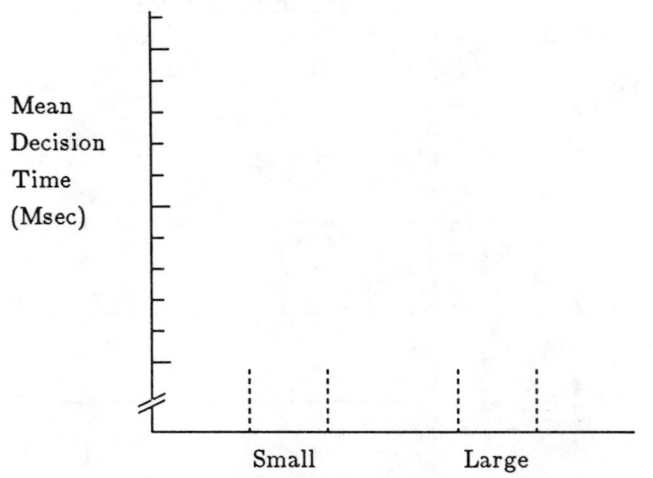

Mean Decision Time (Msec)

Small   Large
Physical Difference between the object pairs

What do the results tell you? If you look at your graph, you should see that the time to make a correct decision was longer for the small level of physical size difference, e.g. ant and flea, and shorter for the large level of difference, e.g. ant and elephant. How did your results compare with that of the rest of the group of subjects? If they were different can you think why that might have occurred? Use this space to summarize your thoughts.

_____
_____
_____
_____
_____
_____
_____
_____

Even though we have hopefully demonstrated a difference in mean score between small and large conditions, this does not necessarily imply that the obtained difference is a reliable and valid one. In order to establish this we need to employ a statistical test of the difference between the two sets of scores. One suitable test would be the *t-test for correlated means* and you should proceed to carry this test out on the data that you have been given. The computational steps are set out below to make this easier for you. You can also refer to any good introductory statistics textbook for additional computational and theoretical information about this test.

Mental Imagery

Computational space to compute a t-test for correlated data
(Matched-pairs t-test)

	Physical Difference			
Subject	Small	Large	D	D^2
1				
2				
3				
4				
5				
6				
7				
8				
9				
10				
11				
12				
13				
14				
You				

$\Sigma D =$ _____ $\Sigma D^2 =$ _____

Notes:

D = The difference between each pair of scores, therefore subtract the reaction time for Large from that for Small for each subject. Thus if the values for Subject 1 were 1200 and 1000, the value of D would be 200.

D^2 = The square of each of the differences. In the case of D = 200, then D^2 = 40000.

ΣD = The sum of all the values of D.

ΣD^2 = The sum of all the values of D^2.

N = The number of pairs of scores (i.e. the number of subjects)

Mental Imagery

Formula:

A suitable formula to calculate t is given below. Use the space provided to substitute the calculated values for the variables in the formula and work out a value for t using a calculator or tables to work out the square root:

$$ t = \frac{\Sigma D}{\sqrt{\dfrac{N \times \Sigma D^2 - (\Sigma D^2)}{N - 1}}} $$

Therefore your estimate of $t =$ _____ ?

We now need to work out if this value of t is sufficiently large to be unlikely to occur by chance, i.e. that it will occur by chance on less than 5 occasions in 100. This is done by calculating the degrees of freedom available, using the formula:

$$ \mathbf{d.f.\ =\ N\ -\ 1} $$

In our case this gives us 14 degrees of freedom and we can turn to the Appendix of a suitable statistics textbook to find the table of distributions of t. This will tell us what value of t would be equivalent to a likelihood of a chance occurrence equal to 5 in 100. We do need to know one additional thing, however, and that is whether we are using a *one-tailed test* or a *two-tailed test*. We decide this on the basis of whether we predicted the direction of effect before running the experiment. In fact we did do so, we argued that the reaction times for the Large condition should be smaller than those for the Small condition and so we can use the less stringent one-tailed test. Looking at the correct table, we can see that for 14 degrees of freedom, and with a one-tailed test, any value of $t > 1.761$ would have a probability of occurrence by chance of < 0.05 (i.e. 5 times in 100). Therefore if your value of t is greater than 1.761, you may safely reject the null hypothesis that there is no difference between the two conditions in this study. If it is not, even if there seems to be a large difference between the group means, you cannot reject the null hypothesis.

Discussion

Hopefully you will have calculated a value of t that is significant ($p < 0.05$) which implies that we can, in formal terms, reject the null hypothesis that there is no difference between the scores for the large and small conditions. We can therefore accept the hypothesis that there is a real difference between these conditions. This is the result that Moyer originally obtained and it has been taken to mean that subjects are probably forming visual images of the animals and comparing these images with each other, rather than using more abstract semantic information. If this is the case, it certainly supports the position that we can use visual images in much the same way as we can use visual percepts.

Experiment Two

Cooper and Shepard (1978) have also tested the validity of this position by demonstrating that viewing an external stimulus and making decisions about it are essentially similar to the processes involved in forming and utilizing internal representations. Their experimental procedure appears to demonstrate quite convincingly the truth of the "internal image" hypothesis. What they did was to present their subjects with a letter stimulus such as the capital letter "F" in a variety of orientations, e.g. 60, 90 and 120 degrees from the vertical. The subjects' task was to decide whether the stimulus was a normal letter "F" or was a mirror-reversal. Generally, subjects took progressively longer to make their judgments, the more the orientation angle of the stimulus increased in extent from the vertical standard. The increase in time with increase in visual angle is usually found to be "linear", that is, there is a constant increase in time with increasing angle. The time to rotate a stimulus oriented at 30 degrees from vertical would therefore be twice as long as that to rotate a stimulus at 60 degrees. This seems to imply that subjects are mentally rotating the image of the stimulus in their "mind's eye" so that it takes up the vertical orientation and can then be compared with the standard (or prototype) for normality or mirror-reversal.

A variation of this procedure will be used in this second experiment in order to determine the validity of Cooper and Shepard's model when geometric rather than letter stimuli are adopted.

Design

This experiment will utilise a within subjects design in which a group of subjects will be tested on each condition of the study. The independent variable will be the angle that the test stimuli diverge from the vertical orientation and the dependent variable will be the median time taken by the subjects to make their judgments about whether or not the test stimulus is mirror-reversed in relation to a standard stimulus figure.

Subjects

You will run yourself as a subject in this experiment and you may if you wish gain experience of running other people as subjects by testing a volunteer who has not previously been tested in this or any similar experiment. After you have finished testing yourself, the computer will provide you with a data-set comprising the results of 14 subjects who have previously completed this experiment.

Stimuli

A vertically-oriented geometric shape will be utilised as the standard stimulus in this study and it will be presented on the left side of the computer screen in one of its two mirror-image forms. The same figure will be used as the test stimulus and it will appear simultaneously on the right side of the screen, rotated a given angular extent clockwise from the vertical on each trial and it may be mirror-reversed or not with respect to the standard stimulus on the left. Fig. 8.2 shows the standard stimulus on the left and one of the test stimuli on the right in its mirror-reversed form and rotated at 0 degrees from the vertical; one of the 8 different orientations that are possible.

Fig.8.2.   *The standard stimulus in normal and mirror reversed forms.*

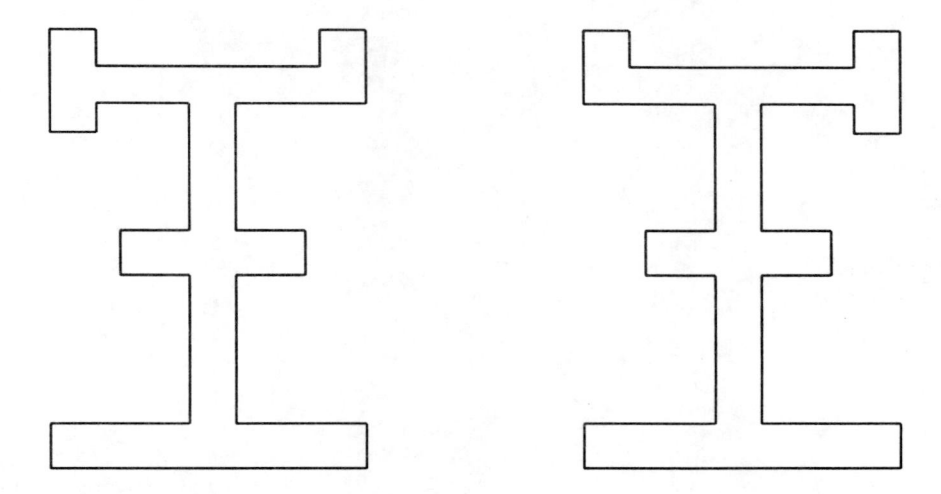

As reported above, the comparison or test stimulus may appear in any of 8 orientations 0, 45, 90, 135, 180, 225, 270 and 315 degrees and may be either normal or mirror-reversed compared to the standard. Thus there are 16 possible forms of the test stimulus in the experiment and each will be shown four times, the order being determined on a random basis for each subject by the computer. There will accordingly be 64 trials in the experiment.

Mental Imagery

Procedure

The computer will begin the experiment by showing you the stimuli on the screen, followed by eight practice trials during which you will be given feedback about the accuracy of your judgments. Each trial will begin with a READY? enquiry from the computer. Once you are ready, press the SPACE BAR to let the computer know and, immediately afterwards, it will present a cross in the centre of the screen followed in a second by a pair of stimuli (the standard on the left and the test stimulus on the right).

Hold your two forefingers (index fingers) so that the left forefinger rests lightly on the "S" key and the right forefinger so that it rests on the "D" key. These keys are on the left of the middle row of the keyboard. As soon as you possibly can press one of these keys to indicate your decision. Press the S key if you decide that the test stimulus on the right is the same as the standard stimulus on the left. Press the D key if you decide it is different – where "different" means mirror-reversed.

Please note that as a result of the difficulty in producing graphic displays on a computer screen there may be minor differences between examples of the shapes in different orientations. However, the only difference that is relevant to this study is one which indicates mirror-reversal. In addition it is important that you remember to make your decision as rapidly as you possibly can, making as few errors as possible.

AT THIS POINT, DO NOT READ ANY MORE OF THIS UNIT. CARRY ON AND RUN THE EXPERIMENT IN CASE YOUR RESPONSES ARE INFLUENCED BY READING FURTHER.

Mental Imagery

Results

After you have completed the experiment, the computer will present your results in the form of median scores for each of the 8 angles of orientation. If you have made any errors, this information will also be presented. Please copy these data accurately into Table 7.2.

Table 7.2. *Median decision times for a single subject.*

	Orientation							
	0	45	90	135	180	225	270	315
Median	___	___	___	___	___	___	___	___
No. of Errors	___	___	___	___	___	___	___	___

Once you have transcribed this information, the computer will display the median data from a further 14 subjects who have completed this experiment. Copy these data into Table 7.3, adding your own results as the 15th subject.

Table 7.3. *Median decision time data from 15 subjects.*

Subject	Orientation							
	0	45	90	135	180	225	270	315
1	___	___	___	___	___	___	___	___
2	___	___	___	___	___	___	___	___
3	___	___	___	___	___	___	___	___
4	___	___	___	___	___	___	___	___
5	___	___	___	___	___	___	___	___
6	___	___	___	___	___	___	___	___
7	___	___	___	___	___	___	___	___
8	___	___	___	___	___	___	___	___
9	___	___	___	___	___	___	___	___
10	___	___	___	___	___	___	___	___
11	___	___	___	___	___	___	___	___
12	___	___	___	___	___	___	___	___
13	___	___	___	___	___	___	___	___
14	___	___	___	___	___	___	___	___
You	___	___	___	___	___	___	___	___
Means	___	___	___	___	___	___	___	___

Mental Imagery

What do these group results actually indicate? The best way to start to analyse them is to produce a graph which shows the effect of orientation on decision time. Take the data in Table 7.3 and calculate the group means for each angle, then enter these points neatly and accurately into the graph provided in Fig. 7.3.

Fig. 7.3. *The effect of angle of orientation on decision time.*

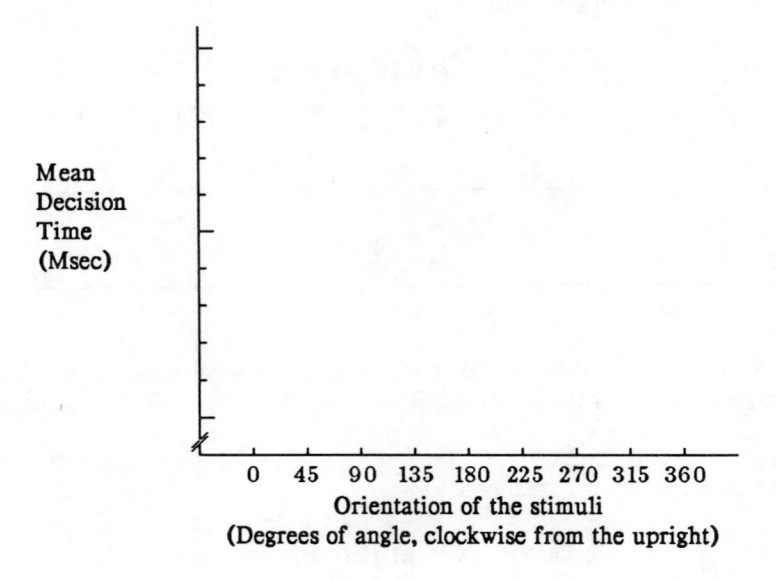

Mean Decision Time (Msec)

0 45 90 135 180 225 270 315 360
Orientation of the stimuli
(Degrees of angle, clockwise from the upright)

As you will already have appreciated, the 0 and 360 degree figures have to be identical and this allows you to use the same data for both points. What then have you discovered from your graph? If your results are like the original ones of Cooper and Shepard, you will have a graph that indicates a relatively steady increase in reaction time as the angle of orientation of the test stimulus increases up to 180 degrees, followed by a steady decrease in reaction time as the angle increases up to 360 degrees. This seems to support the idea of mental rotation of an image at a relatively constant angular speed. You will note that you have not been asked to carry out any statistical test, but simply to make judgments based on a graph. This is simply for convenience in this particular situation. We could have carried out a test such as a *One-way Analysis of Variance* to see if there is an overall effect of angular orientation and followed this up with a number of *paired comparisons tests* of the individual means to see which ones differ reliably from each other.

Discussion

Further evidence for the existence of mental images and the fact that they are subject to the same processes as visual percepts comes from a set of experiments carried out by Brooks (1968). These experiments were based on the idea that we have great difficulty in doing more than one task at a time, with the result that one task will interfere with another. Tasks are held to interfere with each other because they are competing for the scarce or limited central resources that allow processing and thus performance to take place. These resources are held by some researchers to be modality specific, that is, tasks only compete for resources when they draw upon the same sensory modalities. Thus two visually-based tasks will interfere with each other, while a visual and an auditory task will not interfere (or at least will interfere very little). Brooks took advantage of this in his first experiment to give his subjects a visual imaging task coupled with a secondary task - either visual or auditory. Performance was better in the group given the secondary auditory task. In a second experiment, Brooks gave his subjects a verbal imagery task coupled with either a visual or a verbal secondary task. In this situation, the subjects given the two verbal tasks did more poorly. Brooks concluded that the implication of this pair of experiments is that images incorporate information that can be processed in just the same way as direct perceptions.

However, it is probably far too simplistic to believe that it is possible to draw a strong analogy between rotating an image in the mind and the physical rotation of an object in space. For example, a number of factors influence mental rotation that would be unlikely to influence physical rotation. Amongst these factors are practice at the task, beliefs and expectations about the object and the visual properties of the object (Pylyshyn, 1979).

Further evidence that mental rotation may not simply be accounted for in terms of rotation of mental "pictures" is indicated by Carpenter and Eisenberg (1978) who reported that they found evidence of mental rotation in congenitally blind subjects and in blindfolded subjects who were given a haptic rotation task.

On the basis of his research Pylyshyn (1973, 1978, 1980) has argued that images are based on propositional knowledge i.e on an abstract description rather than a picture-like representation. The image is in fact held to be an epiphenomenon. Examples of such descriptions would be IN FRONT OF (RUG, DOOR) which describes a rug in front of a door and IN (TIN, CUPBOARD) which describes a tin inside a cupboard. Any visual scene could be represented by a list of such propositions. Evidence for this type of model comes from a variety of evidence. Consider, for example, what happens when you form an image of a scene. Suppose your image was incomplete, as they often are and you left out an object from the scene. Why do you never miss out part of an object, e.g. like the leg of a chair, instead of missing out the whole chair? If our images were exactly like pictures, we could remove part of any object by tearing a section out. On the other hand, if our images are based upon propositions, then we might expect to miss out whole objects rather than parts.

Consider also the process of forming an image of something that you have never actually seen. Imagine a pink gorilla, wearing a green bra and panties, walking through a town park. You can actually form a visual image of this because you are able to draw upon stored knowledge about gorillas, undergarments and parks to generate a reasonably vivid and accurate image. This stored knowledge is of a propositional nature and is the kind of information that computer scientists have utilized to enable image generation in computer systems.

Other researchers have disputed that propositional knowledge is the fundamental form of representation and that mental images are essentially *epiphenomenal* and have no real function. Kosslyn and Shwartz (1977), for example, have used both propositional and analogue forms of representation in the development of a computer model of the imagery system. Their view is that images are generated from a stored set of propositions. However, they also argue that images have properties which are not contained in the set of propositions that are used to generate them. Take the situation where a subject is asked to make a judgment about the relative attractiveness of two scenes. Each scene can be recreated in the form of an image and the images compared for overall pleasantness, but the global or holistic property of "pleasantness" is not contained within the list of propositions that define the scenes.

Other evidence that the perceptual features of images are able to affect performance comes from Kosslyn (1975) who asked his subjects to imagine various animals and manipulated the instructions to ensure that the imaged animal was either large or small. He then asked his subjects questions about the imaged animal. For example, a cat could be imagined next to a flea or next to an elephant and a sample question would be "is the following feature appropriate for a cat? -claws". The smaller the image of the animal, the longer it took subjects to make an accurate reply. It seemed that they were actually focusing in on the feature in the image and having to scale it up in size where the image was very small. This process took longer than where the image needed no scaling up. It was argued that a propositional system would have the feature "claws" defined in the proposition list -HAS (CAT, CLAWS) and the size of the image should thus have been unimportant. In a further experiment, Keenan and Moore (1979) asked their subjects to imagine described scenes in which objects were either open to view or concealed by another object in the scene. When an unexpected test of memory was given shortly afterwards, memory for the "visible" objects was better than for the "concealed" ones. The authors felt that this could not be explained in terms of abstract propositions.

It could be argued, however, that the act of forming an image requires the subject to draw on propositional information. The amount of information included in the propositional "set" may depend on a number of factors such as instructions to subjects, so that certain instructions or expectations would involve different "sets" being created. The effect of this would be that if greater detail is ever required than is incorporated within the original set, then new propositions must be added. This would take additional time which could explain Kosslyn's results. It might also explain Keenan and Moore's data since it is known that the greater the number of associative links that are available when information is processed, the better the memory for the information tends to be because there are potentially more retrieval cues. It could be argued that the concealed objects required or occasioned the creation of less rich sets of propositions (we might call them impoverished images) than the visible objects. This could have meant fewer retrieval cues being potentially available.

It does not look as if it is possible at present to fully resolve the various issues involved in the study of visual imagery. As a "best bet" it might be fair to conclude that images are stored in the form of lists of formal propositions, but when reconstituted in the form of images, the images may have functional properties that are independent of, i.e. not specified by, the propositional statements.

Recommended Reading

Block, N. (Ed.). (1981). *Imagery*. Cambridge, Mass.: MIT. Although this is an advanced level text, the introduction at least is worth attempting.

Ruch, J.C. (1984). *Psychology: The Personal Science*. Belmont, Cal.: Wadsworth. (Pages 283 and 346-352).

References

Anderson, J.R. (1978). Arguments concerning representation for mental imagery. *Psychological Review*, 85, 249-277.

Brooks, L.R. (1968). Spatial and verbal components in the act of recall. *Canadian Journal of Psychology*, 22, 349-368.

Carpenter, P.A., and Eisenberg, P. (1978). Mental rotation and the frame of reference in blind and sighted individuals. *Perception and Psychophysics*, 23, 117-124.

Cooper, L.A., and Shepard, R.N. (1978). Transformations on representations of objects in space. In E.C. Carterette and M.P. Friedman (Eds.), *Handbook of Perception (Vol.8): Perceptual Coding*. New York: Academic.

Keenan, J.M., and Moore, R.E. (1979). Memory for images of concealed objects: a reexamination of Neisser and Kerr. *Journal of Experimental Psychology: Human Learning and Memory*, 5, 374-385.

Kosslyn, S.M. (1973). Scanning visual images: some structural implications. *Perception and Psychophysics*, 14, 90-94.

Kosslyn, S.M. (1975). Information representation in visual images. *Cognitive Psychology*, 7, 341-370.

Kosslyn, S.M. (1978). Imagery and internal representation. In E. Rosch and B.B. Lloyd (Eds.), *Cognition and Categorization*. Hillsdale, N.J.: LEA.

Kosslyn, S.M. (1980). *Image and Mind*. Cambridge: Harvard University Press.

Kosslyn, S.M. (1981). The medium and the message in mental imagery: a theory. *Psychological Review*, 88, 46-66.

Kosslyn, S.M., Ball, T.M., and Reiser, B.J. (1978). Visual images preserve metric spatial information: Evidence from studies of image scanning. *Journal of Experimental Psychology: Human Perception and Performance*, 4, 47-60.

Kosslyn, S.M., and Pomerantz, J.R. (1977). Imagery, propositions and the form of internal representations. *Cognitive Psychology*, 8, 52-76.

Kosslyn, S.M., and Shwartz, S.P. (1977). A simulation of visual imagery. *Cognitive Science*, 1, 265-296.

Mitchell, D.B., and Richman, C.L. (1980). Confirmed reservations: mental travel. *Journal of Experimental Psychology: Human Perception and Performance*, 6, 58-66.

Moyer, R.S. (1973). Comparing objects in memory: evidence suggesting an internal psychophysics. *Perception and Psychophysics*, 13, 180-184.

Neisser, U. (1982). *Memory Observed: Remembering in Natural Contexts*. San Francisco: Freeman.

Paivio, A. (1971). *Imagery and Verbal Processes*. New York: Holt, Rinehart and Winston.

Peterson, M.J. (1975). The retention of imagined and seen spatial matrices. *Cognitive Psychology*, 7, 181-193.

Peterson, M.J., and Graham, S.E. (1974). Visual detection and visual imagery. *Journal of Experimental Psychology*, 103, 509-514.

Pinker, S., and Finke, R.A. (1980). Emergent two-dimensional patterns in images rotated in depth. *Journal of Experimental Psychology: Human Perception and Performance*, 6, 244-264.

Pylyshyn, Z.W. (1973). What the mind's eye tells the mind's brain: a critique of mental imagery. *Psychological Bulletin*, 80, 1-24.

Pylyshyn, Z.W. (1978) Imagery and artificial intelligence. In W. Savage (Ed.), *Perception and Cognition: Issues in the Foundation of Psychology. Minnesota Studies in the Philosophy of Science, Vol.IX*. Minneapolis: University of Minnesota.

Pylyshyn, Z.W. (1979). The rate of 'mental rotation' of images: a test of a holistic analogue hypothesis. *Memory and Cognition*, 7, 19-28.

Pylyshyn, Z.W. (1980). Computation and cognition: issues in the foundations of cognitive science. *The Behavioral and Brain Sciences*, 3, 111-132.

Schnorr, J.A., and Atkinson, R.C. (1969). Repetition versus imagery instructions in the short-and long-term retention of paired-associates. *Psychonomic Science*, 15, 183-184.

Sheehan, P.W. (Ed.). (1970). *The Function and Nature of Imagery*. London: Academic, 1972.

Shepard, R.N., and Chipman, S. (1970). Second-order isomorphism of internal representations: shapes of states. *Cognitive Psychology*, 1, 1-17.

Shepard, R.N., and Metzler, A. (1971). Mental rotation of three-dimensional objects. *Science*, 171, 701-703.

Shepard, R.N. (1978). The mental image. *American Psychologist, 33,* 125-137.

Wingfield, A., and Byrnes, D.L. (1981). *The Psychology of Human Memory.* New York: London. (Pages 306-316).

Notes

Chapter 8: Reading and Selective Attention

One area of research that has commanded a considerable amount of attention on the part of psychologists is the study of reading. The process of reading is obviously a commonplace activity in civilised modern societies and because of this it is easy to take it for granted. It is only when we come across cases of individuals who have enormous difficulty with learning to read, or who have suffered brain injury, as a result of which their reading skills are affected, that we can really appreciate how complex a skill reading actually is. Apart from the interest in reading on the part of clinicians, many people concerned with education, both educators and publishers of educational materials have attempted to gain some understanding of the reading process.

Much of this research has involved an analysis of the role of eye-movements in reading. It is clear that when we read text we move our eyes in a fairly systematic way around the page, so that with each successive *fixation* we centre a word on the middle of the eye (on the *fovea*) and then we flick the eyes a short distance to the side and centre on a word a little further on. There is some argument about whether we direct our gaze at every individual word or make successive fixations at intervals along each line of text. If we sample the text, selecting the more important words, this implies that we not only take in information at which we are directly looking, but must also take in information from words that are more in the *periphery* of our vision. On this argument, as we read text we would pick out only the most meaningfully important words to attend to directly. Once each direct fixation is made, peripheral vision then guides the next fixation to the nearest critical point. Just and Carpenter (1980), however, argue that this is not the case and that most words are in fact sampled and that when a subject is given text that they can understand, only one-fifth of all words in a text are not fixated and that these tend to be shorter function words such as THE, OF, and A. Just and Carpenter are therefore arguing that while we may pick up information from peripheral vision which helps in the control of eye movements, this information need only be very basic, at the processing level of word length rather than word meaning (i.e. structural rather than semantic). Incidentally, they also point out that our control of eye movements is not always that accurate anyway, with the result that we often underestimate the length of *saccade* required.

There are a number of questions that are raised by these contrasting positions. The most important question obviously concerns whether or not we can obtain information from words that we are not directly looking at and therefore are presumably not attending to. The other questions arise if the answer to the first question is positive and concern how much and what kind of information can actually be obtained from peripheral vision without direct attention. Just and Carpenter's model does not require that peripheral semantic processing is possible, only that some structural information is available. Therefore, it could well be that if semantic processing does occur, then Just and Carpenter's model is inaccurate in some respects, or if it is accurate, that the process of reading text may be disadvantaged by interference induced by peripheral information pick-up.

Early research suggested that we can in fact obtain information from non-attended words in a page of text. For example, Willows and MacKinnon (1973) reported an experiment in which they asked their subjects to read a passage of text which had other words that had to be ignored inserted in every alternate line. Thus in the text which is printed below, the subject would be asked to start reading the second line and to continue reading every alternate one. The lines to be read in this example are printed in upper-case:

> *The moon rose over an incredibly beautiful African landscape, highlighting the dense shrub*
> WHEN THE CLOCKMAKER RAN HIS FINGERS OVER THE HOROLOGICAL
> *which led the eye towards the distant mountain range on the horizon. The senses were*
> EQUIVALENT OF A MASTERPIECE BY REUBENS, THE SENSE OF AWE AND
> *overwhelmed not simply by the visual splendour, but also by the overwhelming sounds and*
> RESPECT WHICH FLOWED FROM HIS EXTREMITIES INTO THE THE LUSTROUS
> *smells of the alien landscape. The cacophony of noise that had earlier stilled to a*
> BRASS WAS IMPRESSIVE BEYOND WORDS. THE AURA OF SOMETHING NOT
> *whispered hush now rose again to an impossibly higher level, while simultaneously the nose*
> QUITE UNDERSTOOD, NOT QUITE UNDERSTANDABLE, WAS CLEARLY PRESENT
> *was marvellously assailed by those so distinctively African aromas.*
> IN THE ROOM AS THE BYSTANDERS GLANCED AT EACH OTHER.

Willows and MacKinnon found that many of their subjects processed the meaning of some of the words in the non-attended lines of text. They assumed this to mean that words that are close to the fixation point can, occasionally at least, be processed at the same time as the word on which attention is focussed. In other words, they are saying that the processing system is capable of handling words in parallel.

Selective Attention

This support for *parallel processing* is strengthened by some research of Eriksen and Eriksen (1974) and Taylor (1977) who asked subjects to make judgements about a centrally placed letter and to ignore letters that were placed to either side. Despite their instructions, the subjects could not ignore the flanking letters and it was clear from their results that subjects processed adjacent letters at the same time as the central target.

Further positive evidence for parallel processing comes from a study carried out by Shaffer and LaBerge (1979) in which subjects were to assign a centrally placed word to a specific category and this response was clearly found to be influenced (made slower) by the presence of a flanking word which belonged to a different category. It is this experiment which we will attempt to replicate in this module, using a method and materials drawn from the original study.

Design

The experimental task involves a group of subjects making a decision about which of 4 categories a target word falls into. The principal experimental manipulation involves placing a flanking word above and below the target word in order to determine the effect of these flankers on categorisation speed. The *independent variable* is therefore the relationship between the target word category and the flanking word category, with 4 levels:

> **Identical word** (same hand responds)
> **Same category word** (same hand responds)
> **Different category word** (same hand responds)
> **Different response** (different hand responds)

The reference to hand response arises because the computer has to be told the category decision that the subject is making about each target word. It is very difficult to learn an association between 4 category names and 4 response keys and so the categories are paired together. This means that only two keys have to be used, e.g. one for Metals and Furniture and the other for Clothing and Trees. While this is a distinct help for the subject, it also allows the experimenter to answer the question about whether a longer response time is due to the different response requirement, i.e. press a different key for the appropriate response to the target and the flanker, or is due to a different processing requirement, i.e. assign target and flanker to different categories. This distinction can be made by comparing the response times to the last two conditions.

For any one subject the computer will assign two categories as the right-hand response and two categories as the left-hand response at random at the beginning of the experiment. Since all subjects will be tested under all four levels of the independent variable, i.e. on all four *conditions* of the experiment, this is a *within subjects* design. The main *dependent variable* is the time to make a correct category decision about the target word, but the number of errors made under each level of the independent variable will also be recorded.

Subjects

You will run yourself as a subject in this experiment and having done this, the data from a further 14 subjects who have previously completed the experiment will be given to you by the computer.

Stimuli

The stimuli are words drawn from a compilation of category *norms* collated by Battig and Montague (1969) and they fall into 4 categories:

> **Metals   Furniture   Clothing   Trees**

Each category group contains 8 frequently occurring words, with between 3 and 6 letters in each. There are therefore 32 stimulus words. The stimulus display itself will consist of a central word, flanked above and below by another word. The flanking word will be the same as the target word in the Identical condition, a different word from the same category in the Same Category condition, a different word from the other category which shares the same response key in the Different Category condition and a different word from a different category which is associated with the other response key in the Different Response condition. See Table 8.1 for examples of the stimulus displays.

Table 8.1. *Possible stimulus displays in the target word categorisation task. In this example the Trees and Clothing categories would be associated with the same hand response.*

	Identical	Same Category	Different Category	Different Response
Flanker	ROWAN	ELDER	SKIRT	BENCH
Target	ROWAN	ROWAN	ROWAN	ROWAN
Flanker	ROWAN	ELDER	SKIRT	BENCH

Each of the 32 stimulus words will be used once as the target and once as the flanker in each of the 4 possible conditions. Thus if ROWAN is a target and ELDER a flanker, then in another trial, ELDER will be a target and ROWAN a flanker. The effect of this is to make possible 128 different stimulus displays and therefore there will be 128 different trials. The order in which words will be presented will be decided on a random basis by the computer.

Procedure

You will sit at the computer trying to keep your head about 15 inches from the screen. This distance is important if we are to replicate the conditions of Shaffer and La Berge's experiment, particularly as regards the size of the stimuli. You will be given instructions on the computer screen and these will be followed by at least 96 training trials which will ensure that you are very proficient at the task before you begin the experiment itself. Detailed *feedback* will be given during training.

Each trial will begin with a request from the computer to press the large SPACE BAR when you are ready for a trial. Once you have pressed the bar, a *fixation spot* in the form of a " + " will appear in the centre of the screen and will be followed almost immediately by the target word in the centre, flanked above and below by another word. Your task is to ignore the flanking words entirely and to decide whether the target word is a member of the category Metal, Furniture, Trees, or Clothing.

In order to facilitate making your response, you will sit at all times with the forefinger of your left hand resting lightly over the "Q" key and the forefinger of your right hand resting lightly over the "P" key. Assuming that the computer has told you that your left hand is associated with Metals and Furniture and that your right hand is associated with Trees and Clothing, pressing the "Q" key will tell the computer that your decision is either Metal or Furniture, while pressing the "P" key will tell the computer that your decision is either Trees or Clothing. The association will be made easier for you to remember, because this information will be re-presented at the bottom of the computer screen between trials. You do not have to remove your fingers from the response keys to start a trial, since you can press the SPACE BAR when required with the thumb of either hand. Please try to make your decision as quickly as possible, but try not to make any mistakes. If you are making errors or responding too slowly the computer will give you feedback to let you know.

After the first set of training trials are completed, the computer will decide if you require further practice before going on with the experiment itself. Once you have reached an adequate standard of performance, you will begin the set of test trials.

Results

Having completed the experiment, the computer will provide you with a summary of your results in the study together with those of 14 other subjects. You should copy this information as accurately as possible into Table 8.2. The computer will give you the response times first, and then the error rates which you should copy inside the brackets in the table.

Selective Attention

Table 8.2. *Median response times and error rates for 15 subjects on a target categorisation task.*

RESPONSE TYPE

		Same Response		Different Response
Subject	Identical	Same Category	Different Category	Different Category
1	_____(__)	_____(__)	_____(__)	_____(__)
2	_____(__)	_____(__)	_____(__)	_____(__)
3	_____(__)	_____(__)	_____(__)	_____(__)
4	_____(__)	_____(__)	_____(__)	_____(__)
5	_____(__)	_____(__)	_____(__)	_____(__)
6	_____(__)	_____(__)	_____(__)	_____(__)
7	_____(__)	_____(__)	_____(__)	_____(__)
8	_____(__)	_____(__)	_____(__)	_____(__)
9	_____(__)	_____(__)	_____(__)	_____(__)
10	_____(__)	_____(__)	_____(__)	_____(__)
11	_____(__)	_____(__)	_____(__)	_____(__)
12	_____(__)	_____(__)	_____(__)	_____(__)
13	_____(__)	_____(__)	_____(__)	_____(__)
14	_____(__)	_____(__)	_____(__)	_____(__)
You	_____(__)	_____(__)	_____(__)	_____(__)
Mean	_____(__)	_____(__)	_____(__)	_____(__)

Selective Attention

You should now inspect these data closely to see if you have successfully replicated Shaffer and LaBerge's experiment. Look to see if the lowest response times are for the Identical condition, followed by the Same Category, with the Different Category and Different Response conditions being the slowest. You should also check to see if there are fewer errors in the Same Response conditions than in the Different Response condition. We can make the results more readily understood if we produce an appropriate graph for the group mean response times. Use Fig. 8.1 for this purpose.

Fig. 8.1. *The effect of type of flanker on category response speed.*

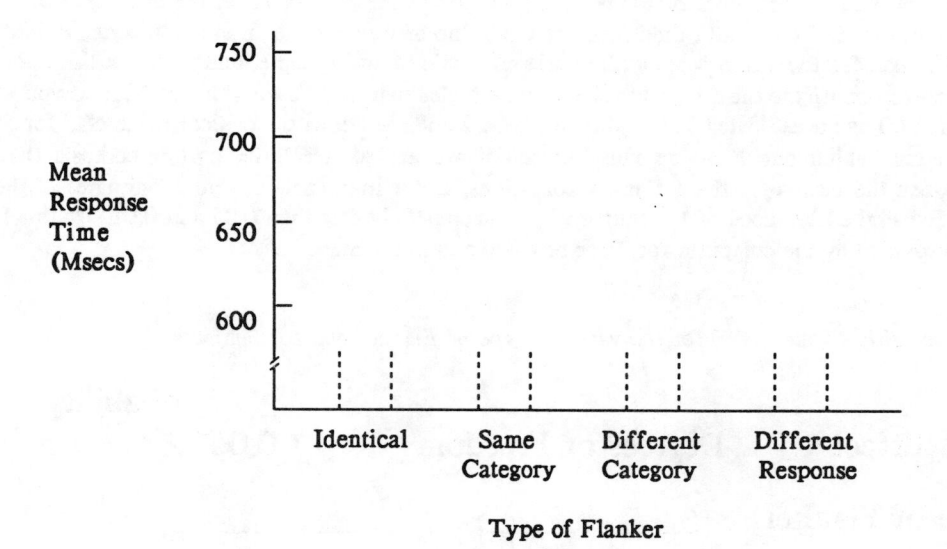

```
                750

                700
  Mean
  Response
  Time        650
  (Msecs)

                600
                     :          :          :          :
                     :          :          :          :
                  Identical    Same    Different   Different
                             Category  Category   Response

                              Type of Flanker
```

While it will often be profitable to assess the trends in our data by looking at summary tables and figures, we require some statistical analysis to be sure that any perceived differences are reliable. In our situation we have a set of results from a single group of subjects th*at are on an interval scale of measurement, where samples are obtained on a random basis from normally distributed populations* and we can assume that the *variances of sample populations are equal*. This means that we can make use of a *One-way Analysis of Variance* (ANOVA) with repeated measures on the same sample. The computational procedure for this test is shown in a variety of statistics textbooks (e.g. Cohen and Holliday, 1982, p. 206-210) and you may wish to attempt to carry this analysis out by hand using the system shown in a textbook. You should certainly turn to such a text in order to read some of the background to analysis of variance testing. In the event that you do not feel able to carry out this analysis, or if you wish to have the correct ANOVA results to check your own calculations against, the computer will present the summary table for an ANOVA which it has calculated on the group data in Table 8.2. You should copy this information into Table 8.3.

Table 8.3.   *The Analysis of Variance summary table.*

Source of variation	Sum of squares	Degrees of freedom	Variance	F
Between Types of Flanker	_____	_____	_____	_____
Between Subjects	_____	_____	_____	_____
Interaction	_____	_____		

Selective Attention

The important values to note are the values of F. You should refer to a statistics textbook and look up the appendix which tabulates the distribution of F. You will note that there are at least two sets of F tables, one for a probability value or *alpha* of 0.05 and another for a probability of 0.01. It is normal to reject the null hypothesis in a psychological experiment if the likelihood of obtaining a given statistic (like F) by chance is less than 5 in 100 (i.e. where the *probability* or $(p) < 0.05$) and so we could simply attend to the 0.05 table. However, we may want to show that our F value is very unlikely indeed and for this purpose we would want to use the 0.01 or 0.001 tables. Having selected the appropriate table, you will see that there are two scales, a horizontal scale with values of degrees of freedom or d.f., and a vertical scale also with values of d.f. What you have to do is to use the d.f. values that you are given in Table 9.3 to enter the table correctly. Let us take an imaginary example, suppose that you have an F value of 10.156 for Types of Flanker, if you look at the d.f. value on the same line of Table 8.3, you might find a figure of 5. You should then look for the value of d.f. for the Interaction term, which could be 62. You should then look for the value 5 along the horizontal axis of the F table, and go down this column until you reach the row corresponding to the d.f. value of 62. Most tables will not show a value of 62, and you should simply use the value for 60 as an estimate. This value would be 2.3683 which is the critical value of F for 5 and 60 (62) degrees of freedom which our F value must exceed if we are to reject the null hypothesis that there is no difference between the means for the 4 flanker conditions. Enter into Table 9.4 your estimates of the values that must be exceeded if the likelihood of F occurring by chance is to be less than 0.05 and 0.01. Do this for the actual values of d.f. provided by the computer for Type of Flanker and for Subjects.

Table 8.4. *The critical values of F for the variable Type of Flanker and for Subjects.*

		Probability	
Effect	Degrees of Freedom	$p < 0.05$	$p < 0.01$
Type of Flanker	(____, ____)	_____	_____
Subjects	(____, ____)	_____	_____

If the values of F that you were given in Table 8.3 are larger than the critical values you have entered in Table 8.4, then you can safely reject the appropriate null hypothesis and argue that your results support your initial hypothesis. Which effects have you found to have associated F values which exceed their critical level?

Having found a significant effect of conditions in this study, we still need to analyse the data a little further to find out whether all 4 conditions differ from each other or whether only one differs from one or more of the others. This type of analysis is often referred to as simple effects analysis and is described in a variety of statistics textbooks, for example, there is a particularly thorough, but difficult coverage in Kirk (1968, chapter 3). The selection of a suitable test is based on well-established principles, such as whether you intended to make the comparisons before you ran the experiment (i.e. a priori), or whether you are simply "snooping" through the data to see if anything of interest comes up (i.e. *a posteriori*). We have predicted certain effects which implied that we would be making comparisons between the 4 conditions and we can employ a test known as the *multiple t-ratio*. The computation of this test is not particularly complex, but the computer will supply you with the results of a completed analysis and you should enter this information into Table 8.5.

Table 8.5. *Significant differences based on the computation of a Multiple t-ratio.*

Condition	Mean	Differences amongst Means
Identical (I)	_____	R-I = _____ D-I = _____ S-I = _____
Same Category (S)	_____	R-S = _____ D-S = _____
Different Category (D)	_____	R-D = _____
Different Response (R)	_____	

* indicates a statistically significant difference between the means at $p < 0.05$
** indicates a statistically significant difference between the means at $p < 0.01$

Discussion

Which differences between pairs of means have turned out to be significantly larger than we would expect by chance? Compare your results with those of Shaffer and La Berge. If we assume that you have managed to replicate the major finding of Shaffer and La Berge, what implications does this have for the reading process? It certainly suggests that it is possible during the reading process for our peripheral vision to detect fairly high-level information (i.e. semantic information or meaning) about words that we are not attending to. It is also possible that at least some of this information may be available to the processes which underlie reading, allowing these processes to direct future eye-movements and conscious attention. In addition, it is likely that we are not aware that such processes are being carried out and cannot influence them even if we are made aware of what is going on. Neither in our experiment or in the previous ones by Shaffer and LaBerge, Eriksen and Eriksen, or Taylor, were subjects able to obey the clear instructions that they were given to ignore certain parts of the stimulus display. This implies that the process of peripheral information collection is an automatic one which is carried out without either conscious awareness or the possibility of voluntary control. There are in fact a considerable number of such automatic processes and the underlying concept is known as *automaticity*.

Are there any other points that we could consider about our data? One thing that Shaffer and LaBerge noticed was that there was a sizable *practice effect* across the trials of their study. Subjects became much faster at the categorisation task over time. How would we investigate this? One way would be to take the median response time for the first half of our trials for each subject and compare these values with the medians for the second half. We could then use a *t*-test to investigate the significance of any difference found. Alternatively, we could add Trial Order as an extra variable into the Analysis of Variance, making it into a Two-way ANOVA. Assuming that we also would have found a practice effect, would you find this surprising? Is it likely to have affected the main results of the experiment? It would in fact influence our main results only if there was shown to be an interaction between the flanker conditions and trial order. Thus, if only the Identical condition showed an improvement with practice, then we would want to modify our interpretation of the results. This was not the case in the original study.

If we have successfully replicated Shaffer and LaBerge and shown that we automatically process non-attended words in text to a semantic level, this has implications for models of reading such as Just and Carpenter's. It could be that this automatic processing is advantageous for reading or it may not be. We can approach this by asking what exactly the flanker is doing to influence response time? Is it making performance on the slower conditions worse (i.e. does it produce an *interference effect*) or is it making performance on the faster conditions better (i.e. does it produce a *facilitation effect*). Shaffer and LaBerge (1979) examined this question in a second experiment in which they looked at a fifth type of flanker. This new type of flanker was a non-word, that is a letter-string such as MIBKS or PIOD and it was assumed that these were neutral as far as any meaningful relationship to the target words was concerned. The general conclusion that was arrived at was that both facilitation and interference were occurring, but that the effect of interference was twice as powerful as that of facilitation.

Since the main effect of flanking words appears to be interference, it is possible that automatic peripheral information selection is not inevitably a good thing. Indeed Willows (1974) has demonstrated that children who are poor readers are more influenced by flanking words than are good readers. The former have poorer attentional focus on the text that they are supposed to be scanning than do good readers, who make use of some peripheral information but are not unduly influenced. Just why there should be large *individual differences* in this respect is not clear, but the influence of automatic peripheral processing must obviously be taken into account in the production and assessment of a valid model of the reading process. A great deal more needs to be known about the factors which influence the degree of interference which occurs. For example, we might ask questions such as how close in spatial terms must a word be to the point of fixation in order to be processed and, does it matter what the case of the peripheral word is relative to the fixated word? These and other questions can be explored using similar methods to those employed in the present study.

Recommended Reading

Carlson, N.R. (1984). *Psychology*. Boston: Allyn and Bacon. (Pages 379-381; 426-430, 468-469).

Roediger, H.L., Rushton, J.P., Capaldi, E.D., and Paris, S.G. (1984). *Psychology*. Boston: Little, Brown. (Pages 157-168).

References

Battig, B.A. and Montague, W.E. (1969). Category norms for verbal items in 56 categories: A replication and extension of the Connecticut Norms. *Journal of Experimental Psychology*, 80, 3.

Cohen, L., and Holliday, M. (1982). *Statistics for Social Scientist*. Cambridge: Harper and Row.

Eriksen, B.A., and Eriksen, C.W. (1974). Effects of noise letters upon the identification of a target letter in a nonsearch task. *Perception and Psychophysics*, 16, 143-149.

Just, M.A., and Carpenter, P.A. (1980). A theory of reading: from eye fixations to comprehension. *Psychological Review*, 87, 329-354.

Kirk, R. (1968). *Experimental Design: Procedures for the Behavioral Sciences*. Belmont, Cal.: Brooks/Cole.

Shaffer, W.O., and LaBerge, D. (1979). Automatic semantic processing of unattended words. *Journal of Verbal Learning and Verbal Behavior*, 18, 413-426.

Taylor, D.A. (1977). Time course of context effects. *Journal of Experimental Psychology: General*, 106, 404-426.

Willows, D.M., and MacKinnon, G.E. (1973). Selective reading: attention to the "unattended" lines. *Canadian Journal of Psychology*, 2, 292-304.

Willows, D.M. (1974). Reading between the lines: selective attention in good and poor readers. *Child Development*, 45, 408-415.

Notes

Notes

Chapter 9: Stress, Life Events and Personality Type

When you sit in an examination hall and look at the question paper in front of you, there is little doubt that you will experience *stress*. Similarly, but more dramatically, if you are tied-up and robbed in your own home, you will, amongst other things, experience stress. This is a psychological state which is correlated with physiological and hormonal changes and it is a natural and indeed often useful response of the body that is related to preparation for extremes of action. However, the situations described are ones that last for a comparatively short time whereas this state can also be created by far more long-term influences such as our housing or employment conditions, and in such instances the stress response can be of much less positive benefit. The first examples are ones of *acute* stress while the second examples relate to potentially chronic stress and it should be mentioned that even acute conditions can give rise to *chronic* stress because of our capacity to recall traumatic events and thus relive the stress-inducing circumstances every day for many years.

What might some of the consequences of stress be? Put at its simplest, *stress can make you ill*. For example, a recent report described the effects of a stressful event on the community of the town of Othello in Washington State, USA. The event was the eruption of Mount St. Helens which caused Othello to be buried under thousands of tons of volcanic ash. Following this event, records showed an increase in the death rate of 18.6% and a 100% increase in *psychosomatic* illness and mental problems. In addition, there were considerable increases in the incidence of child abuse, crimes of violence and alcohol related problems (Adams and Adams, 1984). There are also many reports which have shown the disastrous effects of the Vietnam war on American servicemen (Yager, Laufer and Gallops, 1984).

What are the actual effects of stress in terms of changes in the body? One thesis was put forward by Selye (1976) who believed that the response to stress was fairly constant and occurred in three stages, which in sum constitute the *General Adaptation Syndrome*. The stages are:

a) *Alarm reaction stage* : In this stage, the body senses stress and the autonomic nervous system causes an increase in heart rate and volume of blood pumped, an increase in blood pressure, in rate of respiration and in muscle tension. Skin resistance is lowered. The hypothalamus stimulates the endocrine system to secrete CRF (corticotropin-releasing factor) which stimulates the pituitary gland which in turn secretes ACTH (adrenocorticotropic hormone). Thus within about ten seconds of a stressor's occurrence ACTH will be stimulating the release of fatty acids and increasing the body's utilisation of glucose in order to provide the extra energy that may be required. The adrenal cortex will then be stimulated to release increased amounts of corticoid hormones (such as adrenalin and noradrenalin) and will increase in size. There is a feeling of tension, emotional arousal as well as increased awareness and sensitivity to the surroundings. The individual attempts to cope by immediate physical action and/or by using psychological defence mechanisms. Psychosomatic symptoms associated with this stage include skin rashes, digestive disorders and disturbances of sleep. With very extreme stress, the individual may die at this stage.

b) *Resistance stage* : This stage constitutes the highest level of preparation for action and requires the individual to alleviate their stress by physical or psychological means to prevent psychological breakdown. One problem with this is that in times of stress, people revert to familiar ways of coping and may not be sufficiently flexible to select the most effective strategies. Generally, if coping is adequate, there will be a return to more normal autonomic activity, shown for example by the newly enlarged adrenal glands reducing their size again. However, the body is very susceptible to further stressors, indicating low general resistance, combined with high specific resistance to the original stressor. At this point, many sexually related bodily functions are affected, with sperm production and male hormone production dropping in the male and the menstrual cycle being affected in the female. Both sexes show a reduction in sexual interest (Selye, 1974).

c) *Exhaustion stage* : As a final stage, the individual's ability to cope breaks down and he is mentally and physically exhausted. Before total breakdown occurs, psychological defence mechanisms may continue, but in a bizarre and inappropriate fashion due to metabolic changes inhibiting normal brain function. Physical defences are so low that stress related illness becomes very likely.

However, other researchers have argued that our response to stress is not as consistent as this description implies and that we respond in different ways according to the nature of the stress-inducing situation (Axelrod and Reisine, 1984). What illnesses are most closely linked with stress and how exactly does stress cause such illnesses? One major stress-related illness is coronary artery disease which probably occurs because stress acts to increase the level of *serum cholesterol* in the blood. Evidence for a close relationship between stress and increased cholesterol

Life Events

comes both from animal and human studies. For example, when rats are subject to loud and unpredictable noises, their serum cholesterol levels rise, and when humans are faced with greatly increased work-loads (such as accountants just before the deadline for filing income tax returns) they also show this effect (Friedman, Rosenman & Carroll, 1958). Another major group of stress-related illnesses concern digestive system disorders and include inflammation of the colon, low blood sugar level, ulcers and diabetes. These problems arise from the effect of stress on the kidneys which respond by retaining sodium and fluids. Finally, a variety of immune system problems have been associated with stress and it appears that these may result from stress leading to a reduction in the number of white blood cells (*lymphocytes*) that are available to combat invading disease.

Design

We are going to see if we can demonstrate a relationship between the amount of life stress experienced by a group of students and their subsequent rate of illness There will therefore be two dependent variables, stress and illness, but these will not be manipulated by the effect of an independent variable in this experiment. Rather, they are the end product of a natural experiment.

Assessment of stress

How can we attempt to assess the amount of stress that is being experienced by an individual in order to assess the potential risk to mental and physical health? One way that we can obtain some idea of the stress that people are undergoing is to give them questionnaires to complete that ask them for their own perceptions of the amount of stress they are under. A slightly different method is to identify a set of situations and experiences (Life Events) that are commonly agreed to be stressful and to ask people which of these apply to them. One such questionnaire is reproduced at the end of this unit and you should read through the items carefully. You should think carefully about your answers, perhaps pencil "Yes" or "No" next to each item, and then go to the computer and enter the appropriate answer in response to the prompts that are given.

PLEASE BE AS HONEST AS POSSIBLE

No record is kept of your name or identity in relation to your responses, only the total score is retained. You cannot be identified in any way. Once you have completed the questionnaire, the computer will work out the Stress Rating that is appropriate for your responses and will tell you what it is. Please record it in this space

_____

Assessment of illness

The first questionnaire provided a rating of the stress you faced in the last 12 months. What we will do now is produce a quantitative estimate of the amount of actual physical illness that you have recently been experiencing. This will give us some idea of the extent that any stressful life events in the past are currently affecting your health.

We will use a simple Health Questionnaire to obtain the required information. The questionnaire consists of a list of health problems which you may have experienced over the last 12 months. The computer will present the items to you, one-by-one and you should press the "1" key if you have experienced the health problem once, the "2" key if you have experienced it twice and so on. If you have not experienced the problem, press the "0" (zero) key. Remember that your answers are completely confidential and that if you are going to answer the questions at all, you may as well be honest. No record of your identity will be retained. A copy of the Health questionnaire is duplicated at the end of this chapter.

Once you have completed all the items in the questionnaire on the computer, it will provide a figure which represents an assessment of the extent of any potentially stress-related health problems that you have been experiencing. Please record the figure in this space

_____

Life Events

Results

If your Life Events score is between 0 and 150 then you are not at risk. A score between 150 and 199 represents a mild life crisis situation with a 33% chance of illness, while a score between 200 and 299 indicates a moderate life crisis with a 50% chance of illness. However, the critical value is usually taken to be 300 points accrued, since it has been found that people with higher values than this are 80% more likely to become ill than those in the no-risk category. You may like to consider whether you have had more or less illness than usual in the last few months and whether this may be related to a particularly stressful period in your life (Rahe, 1972).

Relating stress-producing experience to current health problems

We are now in a position to make some kind of assessment of the relationship between exposure to stress in ones life and extent of health-related problems. Obviously we need more data than just your own, and the computer has stored the results of 100 volunteer students and will present a random selection of 14 of these for you to write down in Table 9.1.

Table 9.1. *The total scores on two questionnaires for a group of subjects.*

Subject	Life Events	Health
1	_____	_____
2	_____	_____
3	_____	_____
4	_____	_____
5	_____	_____
6	_____	_____
7	_____	_____
8	_____	_____
9	_____	_____
10	_____	_____
11	_____	_____
12	_____	_____
13	_____	_____
14	_____	_____
You	_____	_____
Group Mean	_____	_____

Once you have copied the information from the screen, you should add your own two scores as the 15th subject. We now need to be able to measure the relationship between the two sets of scores in order to see if they vary together. Thus if the Life Events score is high, will the Health score also be high? The easiest way to do this is to calculate a *correlation coefficient* for the two sets of paired data. However, it usually helps to have a visual grasp

Life Events

of a data set before attempting to carry out statistical analyses and we shall do this by producing a *scattergram*. We can do this in Fig. 9.1, where it can be seen that we are to plot each pair of scores as a single point on the graph. Already printed as a star (*), is a point which represents a score of 100 on the Life Events questionnaire and 5 on the Health Questionnaire. Simply imagine lines drawn from the star to meet each of the axes at right-angles and you should see that these lines meet the axes at the correct points. Now refer to the data in Table 9.1 and put a dot neatly and clearly on the graph for each pair of values. Complete the scale for the Y-axis also.

What you should end up with is a scattering of dots which should be elongated into an elliptical shape sloping from bottom-left to top-right. Please read a statistics textbook to find out a little about interpreting this kind of plot (see the references for suggestions).

Fig. 9.1. *Scattergram for the data from the Life Events and Health Questionnaires.*

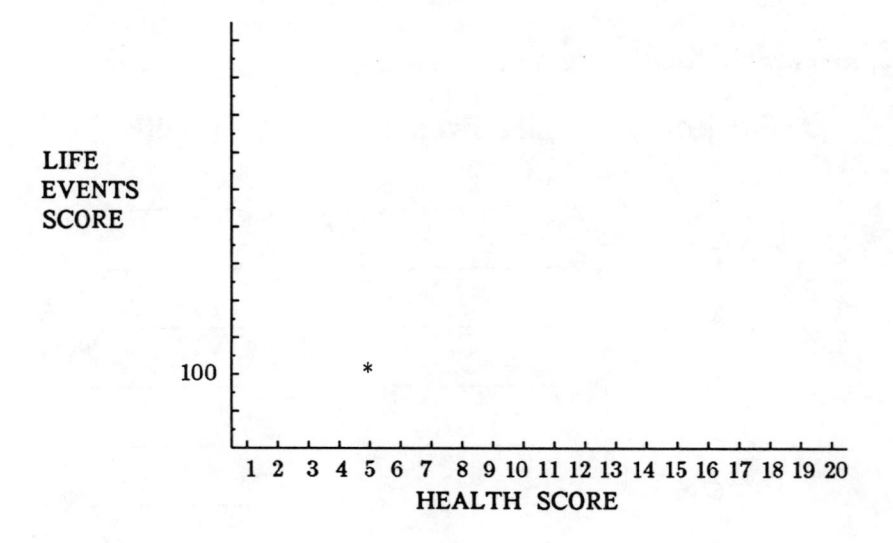

Now that the scattergram has been produced, you can proceed to compute a correlation using a formula and procedure first developed by Spearman. *Spearman's Rank Order Correlation* assumes only that the sample being assessed was randomly selected and also that the raw data are on an ordinal scale. Our data satisfy these requirements and you should be able to calculatehe value of r_s. Why do you think that we did not use a Pearson's Product Moment Correlation?

Carry on and calculate the correlation value for the data set in Table 9.1, using the information provided for this purpose. What you have to do is to take the data from Table 9.1 and re-enter it in the first two columns of Table 9.2. Now take the set of scores for the Life Events questionnaire and rank order them, i.e. find the largest score then the next largest and so on. Once you have done this, enter the rank order for each subject in the third column. For example, if Subject 1 had the 6th largest score, then you would enter the number 6 in the Row for Subject 1 and in the column headed "Ranked Scores - Life Events". You should then continue to do the same thing for the Health scores, so that there are two rank scores for each subject. If you find a tie for any given place, for example, if there are two equal top scores on the Health Questionnaire, then give both of these subjects the sum of the first two places divided by the number of subjects tying, namely two. Each subject is therefore given a rank score of 1+2/2 = 1.5. The third highest scoring subject is obviously given the next available rank order, which is 3. If more than 20% of the scores are ties, a statistical correction should be made, and you should consult a suitable statistics textbook for this information (for example, Cohen and Holliday, 1982, p.154-156), but you do not need to worry about the effect of ties for the purposes of this exercise.

Life Events

Table 9.2. *Rank ordering on Life Events and Health scores for 14 subjects.*

	Original Scores		**Ranked Scores**			
Subject	Life Events	Health	Life Events	Health	d	d^2
1	___	___	___	___	___	___
2	___	___	___	___	___	___
3	___	___	___	___	___	___
4	___	___	___	___	___	___
5	___	___	___	___	___	___
6	___	___	___	___	___	___
7	___	___	___	___	___	___
8	___	___	___	___	___	___
9	___	___	___	___	___	___
10	___	___	___	___	___	___
11	___	___	___	___	___	___
12	___	___	___	___	___	___
13	___	___	___	___	___	___
14	___	___	___	___	___	___
You	___	___	___	___	___	___

$\Sigma d^2 =$ _____

Once you have obtained the two columns of ranks you should subtract the number in the Health rank order column from the corresponding subject's number in the Life Events rank order column. Thus, if Subject one is ranked 5 in the Health column and 3 in the Life Events column, you would obtain a difference score of −2 and would enter that value in the column marked d (d for difference). Following this, square each difference score and enter the values in column d^2 and add all the squared differences together to obtain the measure Σd^2. Given the additional information that the number of pairs of scores is 15 (i.e. n=15), you are now in a position to substitute known values in the formula for r_s:

$$r_s = 1 - \frac{6(\Sigma d^2)}{n(n-1)(n+1)}$$

Life Events

The value of r_s that you have obtained is _____?

Is this a sufficiently large correlation for us to state with confidence that there is a clearly reliable relationship between the two sets of scores? Correlation values can vary between −1 and +1 and we can determine the significance value of our obtained correlation by consulting the appropriate table in a statistics textbook such as Cohen and Holliday (1982, p. 335). If we look at the table for a value of n=15, then we see that:

1. a value of $r_s \geq$ 0.441 is required to be confident the obtained correlation is significant at the 5% level
2. a value of $r_s \geq$ 0.620 is required to be confident the obtained correlation is significant at the 1% level

This means that if we have a correlation value which is equal to or exceeds 0.441, then we can be sure that such a value would occur by chance on only 5 occasions in 100. The values quoted are for a *one-tailed* test where the direction of the relationship is predicted, i.e. we predicted in advance that if the Life Events score was large, then the Health score would also be large.

Discussion

Whatever the result that may have been obtained and there are some researchers who have failed to find a Life Events/Health link (Schless, 1977) there is at least one other major factor to consider. In an important study in America, Locke gave a group of subjects a questionnaire which assessed the amount of stress they believed they were experiencing and another questionnaire which assessed how well the subjects thought they were coping with the stress. Finally, Locke took blood samples and measured the efficiency of the white blood cells in the blood as killers of diseased cells. What he found was that the level of stress experienced by his subjects was not related to the efficiency of the white blood cell activity, but the effectiveness with which the individual was coping with stress was. The implication of this is that two individuals may experience the same amount and kind of stress, but one may cope more effectively with it in psychological terms and his body will be demonstrably less likely to contract stress-related illnesses (Locke, Furst, Heisel & Williams, 1978).

How then can we determine whether we are good or bad at dealing with stress? One interesting suggestion has been put forward by Betz & Thomas (1979), who reported that the individual's personality type may influence his susceptibility to stress-related disease. This suggestion is largely based on the results of a *longitudinal* study carried out by the second author involving more than 1300 medical students. The subjects were given extensive medical and psychological tests at the commencement of their participation in the study and they continued to complete medical and psychological questionnaires every year thereafter (for over 35 years). The results of this extensive enquiry have clearly indicated a relationship between personality type and illness. Three types of personality were identified, called *alpha*, *beta* and *gamma* and the characteristics deemed to be associated with each are as follows:

alpha – Self-reliant, slow, ponderous, cautious, distrustful and slow to adapt to change
beta – The antithesis of alpha, being fun-loving, seekers of new experiences, flexible and spontaneous
gamma – Unstable types, intelligent, but frequently irritable, fluctuating from caution to recklessness and showing a variable self-image.

The least amount of illness was experienced by the alpha group (25% suffering from a serious illness at some time during the study), while the beta group were very similar (only 26.7% falling seriously ill). However the respective figure for the gamma group was 77.3%. How would you describe yourself? If you think you may be a gamma type, do you think you can do anything to change your characteristics or should you just try to relax and accept and like who and what you are?

Another similar line of research has been carried out by Friedman (1969) who identified people likely to have heart attacks as having a distinct personality type which he termed *Type A*. These people are strivers, constantly attacking poorly defined goals in the shortest time possible. The other type that he identified were termed *Type B* and these were held to be relaxed, quiet and calm. Interestingly, when placed in competitive situations, higher serum cholesterol and norepinephrine levels have been reported in Type A's than in Type B's (Glass, 1977) and this fits in with our earlier discussion. Questionnaires have been devised to assess these personality types, see Glass (1977) for example, and typical questions and answers would be:

Question	Type A	Type B
1) Has anyone ever told you that you eat too fast?	Yes, often	Yes, once or twice, or never
2) How would a close friend rate your level of activity	Too active, should slow down	Too slow, or about average

These studies are now firmly within the remit of the new research area of *behavioural medicine*, an area which represents a potentially exciting fusion of medical and psychological research, and within which there is considerable potential for gains to be made for both the individual and for society (Schwartz & Weiss, 1978).

Recommended Reading
Most introductory textbooks cover this topic in some detail. For example, try:
Dworetzky, J.P. (1985). *Psychology*. St. Paul: West. (Chapter 14).

References
Adams, P.R., and Adams, G.R. (1984). Mount Saint Helen's ashfall. *American Psychologist, 39*, 252-260.
Axelrod, J., and Reisine, T.D. (1984). Stress hormones: Their interaction and regulation. *Science, 224*, 452-459.
Betz, B.J., and Thomas, C.B. (1979). Individual temperament as a predictor of health or premature disease. *The Johns Hopkins Medical Journal, 144*, 81-89.
Cohen, L., and Holliday, M. (1982). *Statistics for Social Scientists*. London: Harper and Row.
Cooper, C. (1985). *Psychosocial Stress and Cancer*. London: Wiley.
Friedman, M. (1969). *Pathogenesis of Coronary Heart Disease*. New York: McGraw-Hill.
Friedman, M., and Rosenman, R.H. (1959). Association of specific overt behavior pattern with blood and cardiovascular findings. *Journal of the American Medical Association, 169*, 1286-1296.
Friedman, M., Rosenman, R.H., & Carroll, V. (1958). Changes in the serum cholesterol and blood-clotting time in men subjected to cyclic variation of occupational stress. *Circulation, 17*, 852-861.
Friedman, M., and Ulmer, D. (1984). *Treating Type A behavior - and your Heart*. New York: Knopf.
Glass, D.C. (1977). *Behavior Patterns, Stress and Coronary Disease*. Hillsdale, N.J.: LEA.
Glass, D.C., and Singer, J.E. (1972). *Urban Stress: Experiments on Noise and Social stressors*. New York: Academic.
Holmes, T.H., and Rahe, R.H. (1967). The social readjustment rating scale. *Journal of Psychosomatic Research, 11*, 213-218.
Locke, S.E., Furst, M.W., Heisel, J.S., and Williams, R.M. (1978). The Influence of Stress on the Immune Response. *Paper presented at the annual meeting of the American Psychosomatic Society*, Washington, D.C.
Monat, A., and Lazarus, R.S. (1977). *Stress and Coping: An Anthology*. New York: Columbia.
Rahe, R.H. (1972). Subjects' recent life changes and their near-future illness reports. *Annals of Clinical Research, 4*, 250-265.
Schless, A.P. (1977). Life events and illness: A three year prospective study. *British Journal of Psychiatry, 131*, 26-34.
Schwartz, G.E., and Weiss, S.M. (1978). Yale conference on behavioral medicine: a proposed definition and statement of goals. *Journal of Behavioral Medicine, 1*, 3-12.
Selye, H. (1974). *Stress Without Distress*. Philadelphia: Lippincott.
Selye, H. (1976). *The Stress of Life*. New York: McGraw-Hill.
Yager, T., Laufer, R., and Gallops, M. (1984). Some problems associated with war experience in men of the Vietnam generation. *Archives of General Psychiatry, 41*, 327-333.

Life Events

Student Life Events Questionnaire

Have any of these Life Events occurred within the last 12 months?

Death of a spouse or live-in partner
Divorce
Marital separation or separation from a live-in partner
Death of a close family member or fiance/ee
Served a jail sentence (however brief)
Major personal injury or illness (probably requiring hospitalization)
Marriage
Being sacked from a permanent job (before becoming a student)
Reconciliation with spouse or live-in partner after separation
Major change in health or behaviour of a close family member
Pregnancy
Sexual difficulties (something more than not "getting-off" with someone at the last dance)
Charged with a serious criminal offence (assault, housebreaking, fraud etc)
Gaining a new family member (new baby, adoption, caring for an elderly or infirm person within the home)
Setting up home with a partner (sexual relationship)
Failing examinations and being forced to change University course
Voluntarily changing University course (e.g. from Engineering to Arts course)
Major change in financial position (for better or worse)
Death of a close friend
Change from a permanent job to University student
Major change in the number of arguments with spouse or live-in partner
Obtaining a mortgage for a house
Having the mortgage company foreclose (require repayment of the loan)
Son or daughter leaving home (e.g. to get married or go to boarding school or University)
Trouble with in-laws or parents of live-in partner
Outstanding personal achievement
Wife or live-in girlfriend starting work outside the home
Major change in living conditions but not just a change of address (renovation extension of existing house, deterioration of local neighbourhood)
Major change in personal habits (style of dress, associates/friends etc)
Committing a crime (of more substance than "borrowing" someone's pen) for which you have not been caught
Trouble with Boss, Head of Department, Tutor, Adviser etc
Major change in working hours or conditions
Change of house/flat
Change of University
Major change in the type and/or the amount of sport/recreation
Major change in church activities (going a lot more or less than usual)
Major change in social activities (pubs, clubs, dancing, cinema etc)
Borrowing money for a small purchase (car, hi-fi, camera etc) or to repay a previous debt
Major change in sleeping habits (a lot more or less than usual, or sleeping at a different time of day)
Major change in the number of family get-togethers (a lot more or less than usual)
Major change in eating habits (a lot more or less than usual, very different meal times or very different surroundings)
Holiday (involving travel to a different location and staying for at least a week)
Minor legal problems (parking ticket, disturbing-the-peace etc)

(Developed from the Social Readjustment Rating Scale of Holmes & Rahe, 1967)

Health Questionnaire

Have you suffered from any of these health problems during the last 12 months? (please estimate number).

- accident – major
- accident – minor
- allergies (other than Hay Fever)
- appendicitis
- asthma
- athlete's foot
- backache
- blisters
- boils
- bruises
- chest pains
- cold sores
- common cold
- constipation
- coughs
- dental problems
- depression
- diarrhea
- earache
- eye problems
- hay fever
- headaches
- hearing problems
- hernia
- high blood pressure
- indigestion – severe
- influenza
- insomnia
- kidney problems
- menstrual problems
- muscle strains
- nausea/vomiting
- nervous complaints (e.g. anxiety, phobia)
- sexual problems
- shortness of breath
- sinus/nasal problems
- skin disease
- skin rash
- sleep problems
- sore throat
- stomach problems (not indigestion or ulcer)
- tonsillitis
- ulcer (including stomach ulcer)
- urinary problems
- other

Notes

Notes

Chapter 10: Hemispheric Asymmetry

In most respects it appears that our bodies are symmetrical about the vertical axis, although a closer examination indicates that this is not in fact the case. For example, the two halves of our faces look quite different and if you make a composite face from two left halves of a face and compare this with a composite of two right halves of the same face, there will be marked differences. See Liggett, (1974).

Research into the operation of the human brain has also demonstrated lateral asymmetries and this work is of particular interest because it represents an attempt to associate specific processing operations with localized areas or structures within the brain. At the most general level it is probably true to say that there is considerable evidence that the two halves of the brain are specialized to perform different functions and that at least some of these functions can be located in identifiable brain areas. Many researchers, however, do feel some caution is required in the interpretation of these results.

Most of the evidence has come from work carried out with brain damaged patients and this research has developed from the work of Broca (1861) who identified an area in the left brain which seemed to control speech production, an area now referred to as *Broca's Area*. Broca reported that when this area was damaged in the left hemisphere an *aphasia* resulted (Broca's Aphasia) which was characterized by great difficulty in producing speech. When the same area was damaged in the right half of the brain, no effect on speech could be detected. This work was followed by the research of Wernicke (1874) into damage to another area of the left brain, now known as *Wernicke's Area*. Damage to this area caused an aphasia in which speech was rapid and fluent but was relatively meaningless. These areas can be seen in Fig. 10.1. It is not true that language production is inevitably located in the left hemisphere, but for right-handed people it is true for some 99% of the population, while for left-handed people it is true in some 50% of cases only (Craig, 1979).

Fig. 10.1 *Section of the human brain showing Broca's and Wernicke's areas.*

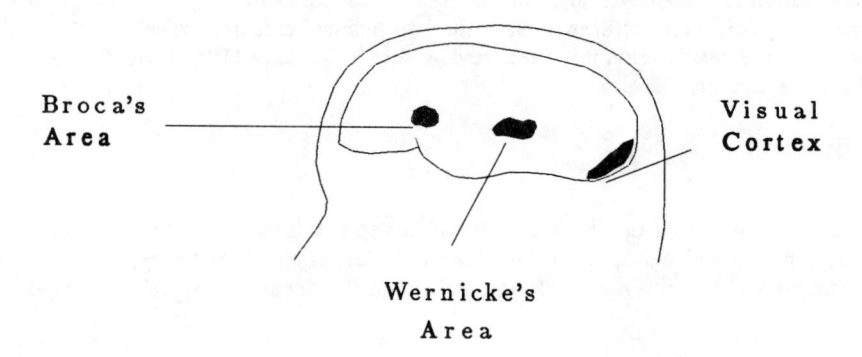

These early studies actually led psychologists to believe that the left hemisphere dominated the right for all types of task, but more recent work by Sperry (Sperry, Gazzaniga & Bogen, 1969) on *split-brain* patients has shown that this is inaccurate and that the right hemisphere can appear equally dominant on a variety of tasks. Split-brain patients are those who have had their *corpus callosum* cut by surgery, usually as part of the treatment of severe *epilepsy*. As a result of this operation the two cerebral hemispheres are separated from each other with no direct interconnections, the only link being via the lower brain stem, and the two hemispheres therefore operate independently. Obviously this represented a marvelous opportunity for research into the functioning of each hemisphere, an opportunity that was seized by Sperry and earned him a Nobel prize in 1981. Functions which have been shown in this research to be specialized in the right hemisphere are face recognition (Levy, Trevarthen & Sperry, 1972) and spatial abilities (Nebes, 1974), while emotional interpretation of visual stimuli and some limited language capabilities have also been found (Gazzaniga & Sperry, 1967).

Of course all the results mentioned were obtained from small groups of very special cases and we would like to know if we can actually generalize these results to the normal population without wholesale and radical neurosurgery. The possibility to gain confirmatory data (or more appropriately to generate disconfirmatory data) comes from the fact that our visual and auditory systems have neural pathways by means of which information from the left half of space is processed by the right hemisphere and vice versa. There is strict division of the neural pathways for sight (see Fig. 10.2), but the auditory system involves more of a 60:40 division of nerve fibres with the major proportion crossing over to the opposite hemisphere.

Fig. 10.2 *Schematic diagram of the major visual cortical pathways.*

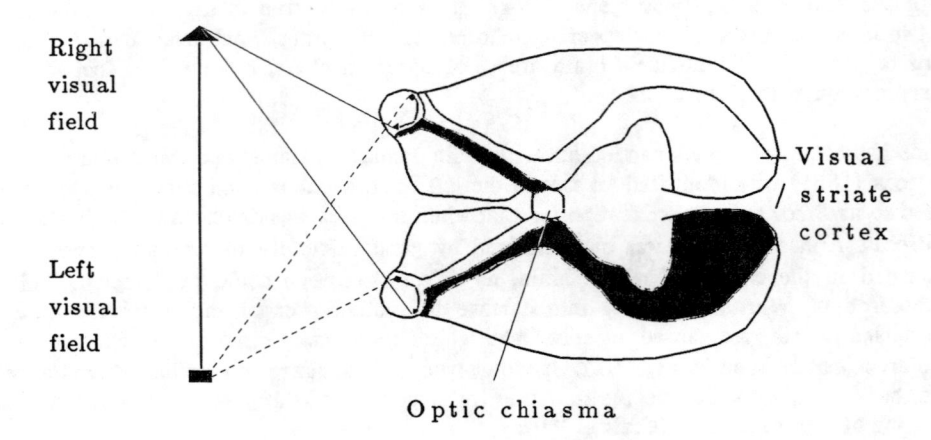

This division of the visual field into left and right, allows us to present information to either hemisphere alone and assess subsequent processing. If for example we use a *tachistoscope* to present a stimulus word to the left visual field for only a brief moment in order to prevent an eye movement (e.g. less than 150 msec) we can ask the subject to identify the word and the time they take to do this should reflect the operation of the right hemisphere. We can repeat the presentation to the left visual field this time and see how quickly the right hemisphere can recognize the word. If there is a significant difference then the two hemispheres are probably not equally specialized for this particular verbal task, a result previously reported in fact by Kimura (1961) who found that verbal processing was much faster in the left hemisphere.

Experiment One
Design
This is a within subjects design in which a group of subjects will be tested on their ability to recognize a series of words following a brief tachistoscopic presentation to the left or the right hemisphere. The independent variable is therefore hemisphere (with two levels – left and right) and the dependent variable is response time.

Subjects
You will run yourself as a subject and you will be provided with the data from another 12 subjects who have previously completed this experiment.

Stimuli
The stimuli are frequently occurring words of from 3 to 6 letters in length. The computer will present 40 words to the right of centre and 40 words to the left in a random sequence of presentation. In order to give you a chance for a brief rest these stimuli will be shown in two blocks of 40 stimuli with a brief pause in between. Each word will be shown for less than 150 msec.

The nearest edge of each stimulus will appear 15 mm either to left or to right of a central fixation spot which will always be on the screen before stimulus presentations to make sure the subject's eyes are pointing straight ahead. It is vital that this spot is always fixated.

Why should the spot always be fixated and can you think of any way that we could ensure the fixation spot is always fixated? One technique we could use would involve on some trials having the fixation spot change for a brief time from a "+" to a number and rewarding the subject for detecting the number.

Procedure

After sitting at the computer, you should keep your eyes at a distance of about 30 cm (12") from the screen at all times and it would help if you used a ruler before each block to check the accuracy of this distance. Your response as a subject will be made by pressing any key on the computer keyboard as soon as you are certain that you have identified the word. Once you have pressed the response key, the computer will ask you to type in the word at the keyboard in order to verify that you were in fact correct. Please type accurately although you will be given a chance to correct misspelling or typing errors.

It may be that on some trials you will not be certain about which word was presented and in this situation you will just have to make a guess. Guesses are often fairly accurate and you do have to make some response for the experiment to continue.

Results

When you have completed the experiment the computer will display your average response times and your error rates for each of the two conditions. Please copy this information into Tables 10.1 and 10.2.

Table 10.1. *Median response times for left and right hemispheres on a word recognition task.*

		Hemisphere	
		Left	Right
Word Length	3	_____	_____
	4	_____	_____
	5	_____	_____
	6	_____	_____
Overall Mean		_____	_____

Table 10.2. *Error rates for left and right hemispheres on a word recognition task.*

		Hemisphere	
		Left	Right
Word Length	3	_____	_____
	4	_____	_____
	5	_____	_____
	6	_____	_____
Overall Mean		_____	_____

Hemispheric Asymmetry

In addition the computer will display a set of response time data for 12 subjects that have already completed this experiment. You should write this in Table 10.3 and add your own data at the end.

Table 10.3. *Mean response times for 13 subjects on the word recognition task.*

	Word Recognition	
Subjects	Left	Right
1		
2		
3		
4		
5		
6		
7		
8		
9		
10		
11		
12		
You		

You should now use the calculation space provided to compute the relevant statistical analysis on the group data from the class. As a guide to the appropriate test to use, remember that you have parametric data obtained from two matched samples (i.e. the same subjects) tested on one occasion.

Calculation Space

Summary statistic:_____ Degrees of freedom:_____

Probability:_____

Hemispheric Asymmetry

Discussion

What conclusions have you reached about the processing time for Verbal material in the left hemisphere (right visual field) as compared with the right hemisphere? Did it take significantly longer to process information presented to the left eye and thus the right hemisphere? Were your own results typical of the group? You can use this space to summarize your findings.

___

Experiment Two

The second experiment has been designed to see if there is a corresponding right hemisphere advantage for spatial information. It is based on a more complex experiment carried out by Kimura (1966).

Design

This is a numerosity judgment experiment employing a within subjects design in which a group of subjects will be tested on their ability to judge how many stars are shown in a brief tachistoscopic presentation to the left or the right hemisphere. The independent variable is therefore cerebral hemisphere (with two levels -left and right) and the dependent variable is response accuracy (number of trials correct).

Hemispheric Assymetry

Subjects
You will run yourself as a subject in this experiment and you will be provided with data from 12 other subjects.

Stimuli
The stimuli for this task are stars which will appear in a variety of randomly selected positions in either the right or left visual fields. On any given presentation there will be between 3 and 9 stars displayed in a brief tachistoscopic presentation of less than 150 msec. The stimuli are random patterns, a possible example of which is shown in Fig. 10.3.

Fig. 10.3. *Example of a random star pattern stimulus in the right visual field.*

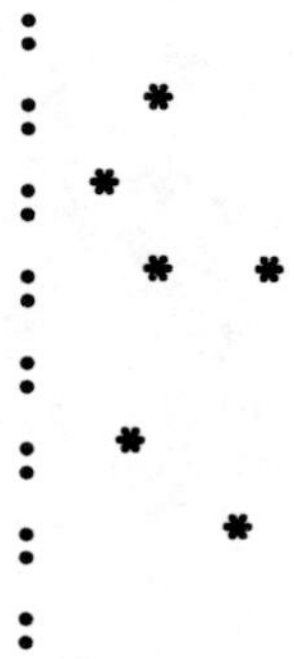

The dotted line represents the imaginary centre line on which the fixation spot would have appeared and the stimulus consists of 6 stars, so the correct response would be to press the key marked 6 on the keyboard. Please remember to keep fixating the central fixation spot and check that your eyes are about 30 cm (12") from the screen at all times.

Results
When you have completed the experiment the computer will display data on your response accuracy. Please copy the information into Table 10.4.

Table 10.4. *Response accuracy for left and right hemispheres on a numerosity judgment task.*

	Hemisphere Left	Right
No. of correct responses	_____	_____
Error rates	_____	_____

In addition the computer will display a set of response accuracy data for 12 subjects that have already completed this experiment. You should write this in Table 10.5 and add your own data as the 13th subject:

Hemispheric Asymmetry

Table 10.5. *Number of correct responses for 13 subjects on the numerosity judgment task.*

Subjects	Numerosity Judgment Left	Right
1		
2		
3		
4		
5		
6		
7		
8		
9		
10		
11		
12		
You		

You should now use the calculation space provided to compute the relevant statistical analysis on the group data. This test will be the same kind that you employed in the previous experiment.

Calculation Space

Summary statistic:_____   Degrees of freedom:_____

Probability:_____

Hemispheric Asymmetry

Draw two simple graphs, Figs. 10.3 and 10.4 to illustrate the group results of this and the previous experiment in this chapter. Use a *bar graph* format and remember to mark your axes and to provide a helpful title for each graph in the space provided:

Fig. 10.3. _____

Fig. 10.4. _____

Discussion

You may not have found a right hemisphere (left visual field) advantage for numerosity judgment. Kimura's experiment has been frequently replicated, but it certainly is a less robust effect than the verbal superiority shown by the left hemisphere. Write a brief Report in the space provided in which you consider both experiments and you make some attempt to address the following questions:

1. In what way might handedness of our subjects have been a relevant variable?

2. What sex differences might have been expected if we had looked at male and female subjects separately?

3. What explanation of better word recognition when words are presented to the right visual field could be offered that relates to our everyday reading skills?

4. Why might an asymmetrical brain have developed in man?

5. Is there evidence from new research techniques such as PET scanning (*Positron Emission Tomography*) which suggests that the brain may operate in a completely integrated way?

Hemispheric Asymmetry Report

Hemispheric Asymmetry

Hemispheric Assymetry

Recommended Reading

Simons, J.A., Irwin, D.B., and Drinnen, B.A. (1987). *Psychology: The Search for Understanding.* St Paul: West. (Chapter 4, pages 84-93).

Hothersall, D. (1985). *Psychology.* Columbus: Merrill. (Chapter 5, pages 171-179).

References

Broca, P. (1861). Remarques sur le siege de la faculte du langage articule suives d'une observation d'aphemie. *Bulletin Societie Anatomique (Paris), 6,* 330-357.

Coltheart, M., Hull, E., and Slater, D. (1975). Sex differences in imagery and reading. *Nature, 253,* 438-440.

Craig, J.D. (1979). Asymmetries in processing auditory nonverbal stimuli? *Psychological Bulletin, 86,* 1339-1349.

Gazzaniga, M.S., and Sperry, R.W. (1967). Language after section of the cerebral commisures. *Brain, 90,* 131-148.

Kimura, D. (1961). Cerebral dominance and the perception of verbal stimuli. *Canadian Journal of Psychology, 15,* 166-171.

Kimura, D. (1966). Dual functional asymmetry of the brain in visual perception. *Neuropsychologia, 4,* 275-285.

Levy, J., Trevarthen, C., and Sperry, R.W. (1972). Perception of bilateral chimeric figures following hemispheric deconnection. *Brain, 95,* 61-78.

Liggett, J. (1974). *The Human Face.* London: Constable. Nebes, R.D. (1974). Hemispheric specialization in commisurotomized man. *Psychological Bulletin, 81,* 1-14.

Sperry, R.W., Gazzaniga, M.S., and Bogen, J.E. (1969). Interhemispheric relationships: The neocortical commisures; syndromes of hemispheric disconnection. In P.J.Vinken and G.W.Bruyn (Eds.), *Handbook of Clinical Neurology (Vol. 4).* Amsterdam: North-Holland.

Wernicke, C. (1874). *Der Aphasische Symptomenkomplex.* Breslau: Cohn and Weigert.

Wittrock, M.C. (1980). *The Brain and Psychology.* New York: Academic. You might like to have a brief look at Chapters 5 and 6 in this book as they provide a detailed look at the asymmetry of language and other functions and discuss split-brain patients. They are not easy reading, however.

Notes

Notes

Chapter 11: Subliminal Perception

A number of years ago, some psychologists became aware of the possibility that man may be able to be influenced by information that is below his *threshold* for recognition, that is, he can be exposed to incoming information that he cannot recognize or perhaps even consciously detect at all, but which can influence his thinking, reasoning and perhaps therefore his behaviour. If this was the case, it followed that man is capable of *unconscious processing* of information and the unconscious as a concept had long been anathematised by many psychologists. However, a growing concern with explaining attentional phenomena was at this time giving rise to theories of attention and memory to which the concept of consciousness had considerable relevance. The extent to which unconscious processing of information was actually allowed for in the various models of attention varied from very little (e.g. early-filter models such as that of Broadbent, 1958) to a lot (e.g. Deutsch and Deutsch, 1963). Over the last decade or so, however, the acceptability of unconscious processing has been enhanced as psychologists have moved away from the conception of perception as an all-or-none, unitary process and moved towards a multiple stage or multi-process model based upon the *information processing* approach. In consequence, most theorists have come to accept the reality of some kind of unconscious processing (see, for example, Broadbent, 1977, for an account of what he terms *pre-attentive processes* and read Klatzky, 1985, especially p42-52, for an informative account of the relationship between the phenomenon of subliminal perception and an up-to-date approach to memory and attention).

Much of the early research interest involved an exploration of the possible practical implications of subliminal perception such as its applicability to advertising. There were a number of attempts to utilise this phenomenon, particularly in cinemas and on television, where simple persuasive messages were implanted in programmes to persuade people to buy various products (Key, 1973). One can imagine the advertiser's dream of people walking to the cinema kiosk thinking "Gosh I'm thirsty, I really feel like a coke, but I NEVER drink coke, why do I feel I must have one?".

Educators also latched onto this area of research and attempts were made to see if it was possible to teach people by playing them tapes of factual material such as foreign language vocabulary when they were asleep. Even governments became interested because if subliminal perception was a real phenomenon, it could be used to influence the population's thinking through the mass media along lines deemed acceptable and desirable. The beauty of this "thought control" would be that people could not even be aware that they were being affected and could not therefore guard against such influence. The principal Western nations have now banned commercial use of subliminal advertising, and presumably they do not use it for their own political ends, but is it in fact a real and powerful phenomenon?

One of the first aspects of unconscious processing to be researched was that of *perceptual defence*, defined as a reduction in the ability to perceive stimuli with extremely adverse emotional associations (Brown, 1961; Dixon, 1971, 1981). Experimentation into this effect involved presenting emotion-related and neutral words singly to subjects for extremely short durations and gradually increasing the exposure times until the test word was reported accurately. On average it took longer exposure times for accurate reporting of emotion-laden words than neutral words. A number of possible explanations for this effect were suggested. The least popular thesis amongst the traditionalists was that subjects guarded themselves against perceiving words that they had not yet consciously perceived. More reasonable suggestions were felt to be that subjects perceived the emotion-laden words just as quickly but were unwilling to report them until they were very sure indeed, in case they embarrassed themselves. To couch it more scientifically, the criterion for detection, or *Beta* in *signal detection* terms (Green and Swets, 1966), was raised for emotion-laden words. Another possibility was thought to be that emotion-laden words were simply less frequently encountered by most subjects and it is well established that frequency of occurrence is an important factor in perceptual recognition speed. However, while there may be an element of validity in both the second and third explanations, there have been experimental designs which have effectively controlled for both criterion and frequency effects and which have still shown perceptual defence. Consider the following experiment by Erdelyi and Appelbaum (1973) in which they tested a group of Jewish subjects. Their task was to detect a set of pictures that were arranged in a circle around a central shape, when the stimulus display was presented for a very short time (less than 250 msec). In one condition the central stimulus was a swastika (negative emotion), while in another condition the central stimulus was a Star of David (positive emotion). The surrounding pictures were more readily perceived in the latter condition which was taken to be evidence of perceptual defence. It could possibly be argued, however, that the negative emotion central stimulus simply captured more attention thus causing subjects to direct less attention to the surrounding pictures.

Subliminal Perception

How else have researchers studied the role of unconscious processes, without having to make sometimes tortuous deductions from indirect evidence? Much early research focused on the physiological changes in the human body that are frequently associated with mental activity. One physiological index that can be measured and displayed by means of an EEG (electroencephalogram) is the electrical activity of the brain. By placing electrodes at particular locations on the head, it is possible to record the ongoing activity of the neural cells of the brain as they continuously alter their rates of electrical discharge. Complex computer analysis can permit the removal of random activity and can pinpoint electrical changes that are correlated with the presentation of various types of stimulus input. Using this technique, some researchers have recorded the brain activity of sleeping subjects and have attempted to show some relationship between changes in brain activity level and the occurrence of verbal stimuli. For example, Oswald, Taylor and Treisman (1960), spoke various words to their sleeping subjects and found that the subjects' own names elicited fairly substantial increases in brain activity level when compared with more neutral words. This certainly seems to support the possibility of unconscious processing.

Further research has concentrated on the electrical conductivity of the skin as measured by the *GSR* (galvanic skin response) which is an *autonomic* response. Experimenters noted that a slight electrical shock administered to a subject was associated with an immediate increase in GSR and they used this fact to *classically condition* a GSR increase in response to certain key words. In the first part of a complex experiment, Von Wright, Anderson and Stenman (1975) presented a series of words to their subjects and whenever the key words appeared they were followed by a mild electrical shock. After a number of pairings of word and shock, the key words came to elicit a strong GSR increase in the absence of the shock itself. The second part of the experiment followed this pre-training and involved subjects listening to a message on one channel of a pair of stereo headphones and repeating it out loud as it was presented to them. This is known as *verbal shadowing* and by comparing what the subject actually says with the original message, the experimenter can be sure that the target message was attended to. At the same time as this message is being shadowed, however, it is possible to play a different message to the subject on the other channel of the headphones (i.e. to the other ear). When the subject is shadowing properly it is usually impossible for them to be aware of the content of this unattended message. In Von Wright's study, the key words from the conditioning phase were either embedded in the attended or the unattended message and when the GSR records from the second phase were examined, they indicated quite clearly that subjects showed an increase in GSR to the key words in either message, although the response tended to be much stronger when the words were in the attended message. The subjects were apparently unaware that the key words had occurred in the unattended passage and this implies that unconscious processing of the key words (and presumably all the other words as well) was taking place. In support of the interpretation that words can be processed unconsciously, it has been reported that synonyms of the key words will also induce a GSR increase in the unattended channel. Thus if the key words were seat, boat and engine, then the synonyms chair, ship and motor would also produce the GSR elevation effect. Since the synonyms mean the same but do not sound the same as the originals, the level of analysis cannot be phonetic (sound-related) but must be semantic (at the level of meaning).

It should be mentioned that there has been some difficulty in replicating these results on the part of some researchers (Wardlaw and Kroll, 1976) and some psychologists feel that it is possible that subjects in shadowing tasks are rapidly shifting attention backwards and forwards between the two messages so that occasional information is available from the unattended message. However, many independent replications have been successfully completed and there is evidence that attention switching is unlikely in the Von Wright experiment (Corteen and Dunn, 1974; Corteen and Wood, 1972). Similar results have also been obtained without recourse to a shadowing methodology by many researchers such as Lazarus and McCleary (1951) who coined the term *subception* to describe this "process by which some kind of discrimination is made when the subject is unable to make a correct conscious discrimination" (p.113).

The present experiment is an attempt to determine the possible effectiveness of subliminally presented visual information, using very brief exposure times of words presented on a computer screen. It has already been demonstrated that words which have had an emotional significance attached to them through shock conditioning can be responded to when the stimulus level is below the normal detection and recognition thresholds, and that emotion laden words such as sexual terms may be responded to by the autonomic and visual systems when the words themselves are not consciously perceived. However, it is also the case that non-emotive words may be recognised at levels of the stimulus that are below those required for conscious perception (Edwards, 1960) and we will attempt to replicate part of a recent experiment which demonstrated this effect (Balota, 1983).

Subliminal Perception

Design

Balota's experiment was a very complex one, involving six different variables (in fact a 2 x 2 x 3 x 2 x 2 x 2 *mixed-factor* design). The essence of our simpler form of this experiment, however, is a consideration of the effect that a stimulus word which is presented just below the threshold for detection (and therefore recognition) has on the speed at which subjects respond on a *lexical decision task* (LDT) involving a target word. The LDT involves subjects making a rapid decision about whether a briefly presented letter-string such as "AWART" is or is not an English word. It has been found that the speed of this type of lexical decision is usually increased by the presentation of a semantically related word just before the target word is shown (Neely, 1977). The first word is known as a *prime* and the expected effects of a prime are shown in Table 11.1.

Table 11.1. *The effects of various primes on the speed of a lexical decision.*

Type of Prime	Prime	Target	Effect
Related	CHAIR	DESK	Decreased LD time
Neutral	XXXXX	DESK	Standard LD time
Unrelated	ROBIN	DESK	Slightly increased LD time

What Balota examined in his study was the effect on lexical decision time of these various types of primes, when presented as *suprathreshold* primes (consciously perceived) and as threshold primes (primes which were presented so briefly that the subject could not have consciously perceived them). He also varied the interval between the onset of the prime and the presentation of the target word. We will concentrate on the single *independent variable* – effect of threshold primes of three types (related, neutral and unrelated) on the *dependent variable* – reaction time to make a lexical decision and the experiment will involve two phases. Phase one will involve a determination of subjects' thresholds for detecting the presence of a prime and phase two will be the main part of the experiment – a lexical decision task where the subject has to say whether the target is a word.

The task we shall use has been designed to somewhat resemble the situation in a cartoon, on film or on a television screen. During phase two of the experiment subjects will be presented with a display like that of Figure 11.1, the difference being that each line will be presented one after the other in the same position on the screen.

Figure 11.1. *Typical stimulus display in phase two of the experiment (each line will actually be shown in the same position on the screen.*

	Display	Duration (Msecs)	
	blank	500	
	+	1000	*Fixation spot*
	@@@@@	40	
	/////	40	
	>>>>>	40	*Pre-masks*
	%%%%%	40	
	=====	40	
TIME	PRIME	Duration P, determined in experimental phase one	
	&&&&&	40	
	<<<<<	40	
	$$$$$	40	*Post-masks*
	-----	40	
	*****	40	
	+	1300 minus P	*Fixation spot*
	blank	500	
	TARGET	*(on till response is made)*	

That is, after a subject presses the space bar to start a trial there will be a blank interval of 500 msecs, followed by a fixation spot lasting 1000 msecs. There will then be 5 frames of non-letter characters at a speed of 25 frames per second. The prime word will then be shown for a duration which will be determined in phase one of the experiment. This will be followed by a further 5 frames of non-letter characters then a fixation spot of duration (1300 minus prime duration) msecs, a blank of 500 msecs and then the target item which remains in view till the subject decides whether or not it is a word.

During phase one, the display will be much the same as in phase two, the differences being that the prime may or may not be present (if not present there will be a blank instead) and that the final fixation spot and target will not be present either, the task being to detect the presence or absence of the prime. The duration of the prime will be manipulated till it is only detected about 50% of the time. This duration will then be used as the prime duration in phase two.

As we must ensure that the primes are presented for as long as possible, but without them being detected and recognised at a conscious level, we will need to determine the threshold for each subject individually at the time of testing, since there are usually considerable *inter-individual* and *intra-individual* differences. A procedure involving systematic variations in exposure time will be employed. The exposure duration of the prime will be controlled by its time on the screen and by the presence of the non-letter masks. A *visual mask* is intended to wipe out a visual stimulus from the visual processing system by "overwriting" the original stimulus in an analogous way to the effect of recording a new section of music over another on a tape recorder. The mask ideally consists of a random pattern of the features of the stimulus which it is intended to blank out. Thus if the stimulus is a word, the mask should consist of bits of letters all mixed up together. One reason that masks are required is because of *visual persistence* which refers to the tendency for a visual image to last for longer than the original stimulus was actually presented so that the subject could be looking at an icon or image of the stimulus for perhaps 100 msec when the stimulus itself was only there for 60 msec.

Subjects

You will run yourself as a subject in this experiment and the computer will provide you with data from another 14 subjects who have previously completed this experiment.

Stimuli

There are 192 letter strings used in this experiment. There are 48 target words and for each target word there is a related prime, an unrelated prime and an associated non-word target. The target words and related primes were drawn from published sets of word association norms (Postman and Keppel, 1970, Ch. 2), each target being the most frequent association to its respective related prime. The unrelated primes were words which did not occur as related to the targets or related primes in the norms and which the current authors decided were unrelated to the targets. The non-word targets were versions of the word targets with one or two letters changed. The median frequency of occurrence of the 48 targets was 79 per million, the median frequency of occurrence of the related primes was 62 per million and the median frequency of occurrence of the unrelated primes was 58 per million words according to the norms of Kucera and Francis (1967). The mean word lengths of the word and the non-word targets were each 4.75 letters and the mean word lengths of the related primes and the unrelated primes were each 4.85 letters.

In phase two of the experiment, there will be 96 trials. The computer will pick 48 target words at random together with 48 associated non-word targets. 16 of these target words will be preceded by a related prime, 16 by an unrelated prime and 16 by a neutral prime. Similarly each non-word target will be preceded by the same primes as its associated word. Table 11.2 illustrates this.

Table 11.2. *Word and non-word trials as a function of type of prime.*

	Condition	Example of Prime	Example of Target	No. of Trials
Words	Related	GLASS	MILK	16
	Neutral	XXXXX	MILK	16
	Unrelated	BRAIN	MILK	16
Non-Words	Related	GLASS	MOLP	16
	Neutral	XXXXX	MOLP	16
	Unrelated	BRAIN	MOLP	16

The words used in phase one of the experiment will be drawn from the list of unrelated primes which are not used in phase two.

Procedure

Phase One: You will sit at the computer and read the instructions for this unit. Your threshold level for word detection will then be assessed. The computer will tell you to rest your left forefinger lightly over the " W " key and your right forefinger lightly over the " N " key and when you have done this and are ready you should press the large SPACE BAR with your thumb to tell the computer to start a trial. A fixation point in the form of a cross "+" will appear in the centre of the screen and you should keep looking directly at this. Keep your head as still as possible and maintain your eyes at a distance of about 24" (30cm) from the screen. After a second or so the cross will be replaced by a pattern of mask characters which will change at the rate of 25 frames per second. In the middle of this sequence there will be presented either a word or a blank. Your task is to decide if a word was presented or not. Press the W (Word present) key if you think a word was presented and the N (No word present) key if you do not think it was. You should press the "Word" key even if you did not recognize the word but thought that a word was there. Once you have done this the first time, the sequence will be repeated by your pressing the SPACE BAR and will be continued until the computer tells you that your threshold has been estimated. This should take between 5 and 15 minutes. Remember this phase is not testing your reaction speed. Take your time and wait till all the flashes have stopped before pressing the key. You should be fairly sure that you saw a word before pressing W. If you are not sure then press N.

Phase Two: The second part of the experiment will follow directly on from the first and will involve a very similar procedure. This time though there will always be a word present in the middle of the masks even if you can't see it - so your decision is not based on its presence or absence. When the flashing frames of characters stop, there will be a second fixation spot and then a target string which will stay on the screen till you respond. You have to make a decision about this target string.

The computer will tell you that it is ready to start the test session and you will let it know that you are ready by pressing the SPACE BAR. Your forefingers should once again be covering the "W" and "N" keys, although this time the decision is between Word and Non-word rather than Word present and No word present. Once you press the SPACE BAR, the fixation spot will appear followed almost immediately by a series of flashes, within which the prime will be embedded. This will be followed by the fixation spot again and then the letter-string target for 2 seconds. You *MUST* look carefully at the display at all times. As soon as you possibly can after the letter-string appears, press either the W or the N key to tell the computer whether the final letter-string was or was not a word. Do react quickly, but you should also remember to try not to make any errors. Remember, especially as you start phase two, that you will be making a decision about the final letter string and not about the presence of the prime.

Subliminal Perception

Results

Once you have completed the experiment, a summary of your results will be presented to you and you should copy this information into Table 11.3.

Table 11.3. *Lexical decision times and error rates for a single subject.*

	Type of Prime		
	Related	**Neutral**	**Unrelated**
Median of all Trials	_____	_____	_____
Percentage of Errors	_____	_____	_____

After you have copied these data, you will be given the lexical decision times for 14 other subjects which you should copy into Table 11.4 as accurately as possible.

Table 11.4. *Median lexical decision times for a group of subjects.*

Subject	**Related**	**Type of Prime** **Neutral**	**Unrelated**
1	_____	_____	_____
2	_____	_____	_____
3	_____	_____	_____
4	_____	_____	_____
5	_____	_____	_____
6	_____	_____	_____
7	_____	_____	_____
8	_____	_____	_____
9	_____	_____	_____
10	_____	_____	_____
11	_____	_____	_____
12	_____	_____	_____
13	_____	_____	_____
14	_____	_____	_____
You	_____	_____	_____
Group Mean	_____	_____	_____

Subliminal Perception

You should now calculate the group means for each type of prime and plot this information in graphical form in Fig. 11.2. The bar-graph format has already been prepared for you.

Fig. 11.2. *The effect of 3 types of threshold prime on lexical decision speed.*

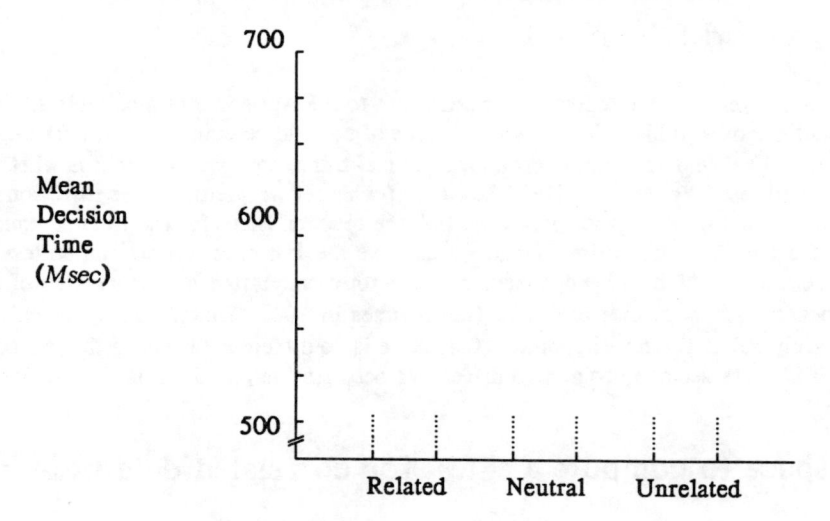

Mean Decision Time (*Msec*)

Related   Neutral   Unrelated

What do the results tell you? If you obtained results like those of Balota then you should have found that it took less time to make a lexical decision when the letter-string was preceded by a related prime than when it was preceded by either a neutral or an unrelated prime. The graph should make this clear and you can refer back to Table 11.4 to see how your results compare with that of the rest of the group of subjects? If they were different can you think of any reasons why that might be?

Even though we have hopefully demonstrated a difference in mean score between conditions involving related primes and those involving neutral and unrelated primes, this does not necessarily imply that any differences are reliable and valid. In order to establish this we need to employ a statistical test of the difference between the sets of scores. Since we have three sets of scores to compare, the most suitable test is probably a *repeated-measures Analysis of Variance (ANOVA)*, the computational procedure for which is set out in a number of statistics textbooks such as Cohen and Holliday (1982). You may not feel confident performing this analysis by hand and since there is really only one critical comparison as far as we are concerned in this unit, it is possible to perform a pair-wise comparison test instead. One such test would be the *t-test for correlated means* and if you do not wish to attempt an ANOVA on all the data, you should proceed to carry out a *t*-test on the data that you have been given, comparing the sets of mean scores for the related primes with the mean scores for the unrelated primes. To make this easier for you, the computational steps are set out below and there is computational space overleaf. You can also refer to any good introductory statistics textbook for additional computational and theoretical information about this test.

Formula

A suitable formula to calculate *t* is given below. Use the space provided on the next page to substitute the calculated values for the variables in the formula, and work out a value for *t* using a calculator or tables to obtain the square root:

$$t = \frac{\Sigma D}{\sqrt{\dfrac{N \Sigma D^2 - (\Sigma D)^2}{N - 1}}}$$

Subliminal Perception

Therefore your estimate of t is,   t = _____?

We now need to decide if this value of t is sufficiently large to be unlikely to occur by chance, i.e. that it will occur by chance on less than 5 occasions in 100. This is done by calculating the degrees of freedom available, using the formula:

$$\text{d.f.} = N - 1$$

In our case this gives us 14 degrees of freedom and we can turn to the Appendix of a suitable statistics textbook to find the table of distributions of t. This will tell us what value of t would be equivalent to a likelihood of a chance occurrence equal to 5 in 100. We do need to know one additional thing, however, and that is whether we are using a one-tailed or a two-tailed test. We decide this on the basis of whether we predicted the direction of effect before running the experiment. In fact we did do so, we argued that the reaction times for the Related condition should be smaller than those for the Unrelated condition and so we can use the less stringent one-tailed test. Looking at the correct table, we can see that for 14 degrees of freedom, and with a one-tailed test, any value of $t > 1.761$ would have a probability of occurrence by chance of < 0.05 (i.e. 5 times in 100). Therefore if your value of t is greater than 1.761, you may safely reject the null hypothesis that there is no difference between the two conditions in this study. If it is not, even if there seems to be a large difference between the group means, you cannot reject the null hypothesis.

Computational space to compute a t-test for correlated data (Matched-pairs t-test)

Subject	Type of Prime Related	Unrelated	D	D²
1	_____	_____	_____	_____
2	_____	_____	_____	_____
3	_____	_____	_____	_____
4	_____	_____	_____	_____
5	_____	_____	_____	_____
6	_____	_____	_____	_____
7	_____	_____	_____	_____
8	_____	_____	_____	_____
9	_____	_____	_____	_____
10	_____	_____	_____	_____
11	_____	_____	_____	_____
12	_____	_____	_____	_____
13	_____	_____	_____	_____
14	_____	_____	_____	_____
You	_____	_____	_____	_____

$\Sigma D =$ _____ $\Sigma D^2 =$ _____

Note:

D = The difference between each pair of scores, therefore subtract the reaction time for Large from that for Small for each subject. Thus if the values for Subject 1 were 1200 and 1000, the value of **D** = 200.

D² = The square of each of the differences. In the case of **D** = 200, then **D²** = 40000.

D = The sum of all the values of **D**.

D² = The sum of all the values of **D²**.

N = The number of pairs of scores (i.e. the number of subjects)

Discussion

Hopefully your results will support the earlier data of Balota (1983) which found semantic priming effects with threshold level and suprathreshold level stimuli. Balota explained these results in terms of a model of the *lexicon* (mental dictionary of words, or semantic memory) suggested by Posner and Snyder (1975). The words that we know and have stored in permanent memory are believed to be organized in a systematic fashion, such that related words have connections with each other. The closer any two words are in meaning, the closer or stronger the links between them will be. The process of recognizing a word is believed to be analogous to activating the internal representation of that word and very quickly this activation spreads along the established links and partially activates related words. It is this partial activation or pre-activation that leads to faster recognition of a word by a related prime. The same process is held to occur whether the prime is presented above or just below the recognition threshold.

A further assumption that has been made by Marcel and Patterson (1978) as well as Allport (1977) is that when a stimulus is presented to the cognitive system, a number of independent processes are automatically triggered-off. Thus a word will be analysed in terms of a visual coding system, a *phonetic* coding system and a semantic coding system amongst others and eventually all these codes are reintegrated at a late stage in the processing system and the result fed into consciousness. These researchers would argue that the only difference between the threshold and suprathreshold situations is that the visual mask in the threshold condition prevents the visual processing of the incoming information. Other types of analysis remain unaffected, however, and the prime is processed into its constituent *phonemes* and is processed for meaning (semantic processing) but obviously when the various codes are brought together for directing to conscious awareness, there is no visual code and therefore no conscious visual experience.

While this explains a good deal it is obviously not the whole story and much remains to be understood. For example, Balota reported that his subjects responded more quickly in recognizing a word that had been primed at threshold than one that had been primed above threshold (a mean of 562 msec as opposed to 726 msec). The explanation for this requires a model of the human attentional system that regards us as having a limited amount of attention that we can apply to different processes at any one time. The process of directing this attention in conscious perception (e.g. in recognizing the prime) takes time and in a sense interferes with the process of recognizing the target word itself.

Some practical aspects of the study also require consideration. For example, many early experiments into threshold effects were criticized for their failure to establish a reliable threshold level for each subject. Thus, Merikle (1982) has pointed out that thresholds will decrease across the first 30 minutes or more of a test session as processes such as *dark adaptation* come into operation and that a response bias on the part of subjects towards saying No rather than Yes can produce a falsely high threshold estimate. As a result of these potential problems, Balota used a threshold estimation procedure devised by Fowler, Wolford, Slade and Tassinary (1981) which lasted some 35 minutes. In our study we could not really permit ourselves the luxury of such an extensive pre-test period and we allowed only 10-15 minutes for threshold estimation. This was obviously not ideal. As a result of this it could be argued that some of our subjects may have consciously perceived at least some of the primes. However, none of the subjects who have been run on this procedure have reported being able to see any of the primes during phase two of the experiment. Did you think that you detected, let alone were able to perceive, any of the primes?

Are you convinced about the reality of subliminal perception? Perhaps you realise now that the layman's ideas on the subject have been at least a little naive. There is certainly a place for the phenomenon within current information processing models of the cognitive system, but it is unlikely that the original flush of enthusiasm for subliminal perception by various interested groups was totally warranted. The subliminal perception phenomenon is not very robust and requires the most careful experimental control to demonstrate it in the laboratory, let alone to use it in any practical way. As far as subliminal perception within advertising is concerned, we could well be better off, as some sceptical authorities have said, if all advertising were subliminal and thus below our detection and recognition thresholds. In consequence, we might not have to consciously suffer the frequent inanities of current advertising practice. Goldiamond (1966) spoke for many psychologists when he said "the advertiser may be saving me the trouble of turning him down" (p.279).

Recommended Reading

Dixon, N.F. (1981). *Preconscious Processing.* Chichester: Wiley.

Roediger, H.L., Rushton, J.P., Capaldi, E.D., and Paris, S.G. (1984). *Psychology.* Boston: Little, Brown. (Pages 155-168).

References

Allport, D.A. (1977). On knowing the meaning of words we are unable to report. The effects of visual masking. In S. Dornic (Ed.), *Attention and Performance VI.* Hillsdale, N.J.: Erlbaum.

Balota, D.A. (1983). Automatic semantic activation and episodic memory encoding. *Journal of Verbal Learning and Verbal Behaviour, 22,* 88-104.

Broadbent, D.A. (1958). *Perception and Communication.* London: Pergamon.

Broadbent, D.A. (1977). The hidden preattentive process. *American Psychologist, 32,* 109-118.

Brown, W.P. (1961). Conceptions of perceptual defence. *British Journal of Psychology Monographs,* Supplement No. 35.

Cohen, L., and Holliday, M. (1982). *Statistics for Social Scientists.* London: Harper and Row.

Corteen, R.S., and Dunn, D. (1974). Shock-associated words in a nonattended message: A test for momentary awareness. *Journal of Experimental Psychology, 102,* 1143-1144.

Corteen, R.S., and Wood, B. (1972). Autonomic responses to shock-associated words in a unattended channel. *Journal of Experimental Psychology, 94,* 308-313.

Deutsch, J.A., and Deutsch, D. (1963). Attention: some theoretical considerations. *Psychological Review, 70,* 80-90.

Dixon, N.F. (1971). *Subliminal Perception: The Nature of a Controversy,* New York, McGraw Hill.

Dixon, N.F. (1981). *Preconscious Processing.* Chichester: Wiley.

Edwards, A.E. (1960). Subliminal tachistoscopic perception as a function of threshold method. *Journal of Psychology, 50,* 139-144.

Erdelyi, M.H. (1974). A new look at the new look: perceptual defense and vigilance. Psychological Review, 81, 1-25.

Erdelyi, M.H., and Appelbaum, A.G. (1973). Cognitive masking: the disruptive effect of an emotional stimulus upon the perception of contiguous neutral items. *Bulletin of the Psychonomic Society, 1,* 59-61.

Eysenck, M.W. (1984). *A Handbook of Cognitive Psychology.* Hillsdale, N.J.: Lawrence Erlbaum. (Pages 24-26).

Fowler, C.A., Wolford, G., Slade, R., and Tassinary, L. (1981). Lexical access with and without awareness. *Journal of Experimental Psychology: General, 110,* 341-362.

Goldiamond, I. (1966). Statement on subliminal advertising. In R. Ulrich, T. Stachnick, and J. Mabry (Eds.), *Control of Human Behavior.* Glenview, Ill.: Scott, Foresman.

Green, D.M., and Swets, J.A. (1966). *Signal Detection Theory and Psychophysics.* New York: Wiley.

Key, W.B. (1973). *Subliminal Seduction: Ad Media's Manipulation of a not so Innocent America.* New York: Signet.

Klatzky, R.L. (1985). *Memory and Awareness.* New York: Freeman.

Kucera, H., and Francis, W.N. (1967). *Computational Analysis of Present Day American English.* Providence, R.I.: Brown University.

Lazarus, R.S., and McCleary, R.A. (1951). Autonomic discrimination without awareness: a study of subception. *Psychological Review, 58,* 113-122. (Reprinted in M.D. Vernon (Ed.), *Experiments in Visual Perception.* London: Penguin, 1970).

Marcel, A.J. (1980). Conscious and preconscious recognition of polysemous words: locating the selective effects of prior verbal context. In R.S. Nickerson (Ed.), *Attention and Performance VIII.* Hillsdale, N.J.: Lawrence Erlbaum.

Marcel, A.J., and Patterson, K.E. (1978). Word recognition and production: reciprocity in clinical and normal studies. In J. Requin (Ed.), *Attention and Performance VII*. Hillsdale, N.J.: Lawrence Erlbaum.

Merikle, P.M. (1982). Unconscious perception revisited. *Perception and Psychophysics, 31*, 298-301.

Neely, J.H. (1977). Semantic priming and retrieval from lexical memory: Roles of inhibitionless spreading activation and limited capacity attention. *Journal of Experimental Psychology: General, 106*, 226-254.

Oswald, I., Taylor, A.M., and Treisman, M. (1960). Discriminative responses to stimulation during sleep. *Brain, 83*, 440-453.

Posner, M.I. and Snyder, C.R.R. (1975). Attention and cognitive control. In R.L. Solso (Ed.), *Information Processing and Cognition: The Loyola Symposium*. Hillsdale, N.J.: Lawrence Erlbaum.

Postman, L., and Keppel, K. (1970). *Norms of Word Association*. London: Academic Press.

Von Wright, J.M., Anderson, K., and Stenman, U. (1975). Generalisation of conditioned GSRs in dichotic listening. In P.M.A. Rabbitt and S. Dornic (Eds.), *Attention and Performance V*. New York: Academic.

Wardlaw, K.A., and Kroll, N.E.A. (1976). Autonomic responses to shock-associated words in a nonattended message: A failure to replicate. *Journal of Experimental Psychology: Human Perception and Performance, 2*, 357-360.

Notes

Glossary

A

Absolute threshold The minimum amount of energy required by a subject for him to detect the presence of a stimulus. See threshold.

Acute Coming to a crisis point, as opposed to chronic.

Adaptation A period of prolonged exposure to an unvarying stimulus, after which the subject usually experiences some kind of sensory distortion such as an after-image. For example, when a subject looks at a patch of red for a period of several minutes and then looks at a neutral patch of grey, he will usually experience the sensation of the complementary colour green, rather than grey. There are two types of after-image or after-effect, positive and negative. The more common type is the negative after-effect where the experience is opposite to the adapting stimulus (e.g. red/green). The positive after-effect is of the same type as the adapting stimulus (e.g. when a bright flash illuminates a stimulus very briefly, the after-effect will be a visual image of the original stimulus as it was originally seen). Adaptation is believed to be largely the result of the fatigue of neural receptors and therefore to indicate the presence of such receptors for any type of stimulus where adaptation after-effects are found.

Adrenal cortex A gland in the endocrine system which is located above the kidneys and secretes several hormones. Some of these assist the body with vigorous exercise by increasing the available blood supply and helping supply nutrients to the muscles, while others are sex hormones.

After-image See *adaptation*.

Analysis of Variance (ANOVA) This is a statistical test of the null hypothesis that three or more populations have the same mean. If we can reject the null hypothesis this indicates that not all of the means are equal. This test can be used in a situation where there is only one independent variable i.e. only one factor and this is called one-way analysis of variance. It can also be used in the more complex situation where there are two or more independent variables or factors. These are called factorial designs. ANOVA's are parametric tests and the data must satisfy the appropriate criteria. Different forms of the ANOVA are used for a within subjects (i.e. a *repeated measures*) design than for a between subjects or a mixed design.

Aphasia Loss of a language function as a result of disease or brain injury.

A posteriori Sometimes referred to as post hoc. In statistical testing, this refers to a class of multiple comparison tests the use of which is decided upon after a major analysis such as an ANOVA is undertaken. It involves "data-snooping" or looking to see what might be found after an F test is carried out. Typical of such tests are the Fisher LSD test, the Tukey HSD test and the Scheffe test. The essential factor is that the specific comparisons being made were not planned in advance. See a priori.

A priori Strictly, before the event. Usually this refers to multiple comparison tests which are used to look at particular effects that were specified in advance of carrying out an ANOVA. The element of prediction allows a less stringent test to be adopted when specific hypotheses are being tested. Examples are Dunn's Multiple Comparison test and Multiple t-tests.

Arithmetic mean See *Mean*.

Attribution A psychosocial process by which we assign cause to event or a personality characteristic to an individual.

Automaticity The process by which, through practice, the mental "effort" required to carry out a given set of operations is reduced to a minimal level and may even be carried out without any mental awareness.

Autonomic nervous system The division of the nervous system which controls the operation of internal organs (including blood vessels, endocrine and sweat glands). It is subdivided into the sympathetic and parasympathetic systems. The former acts to prepare the body for violent activity while the latter reinstates normal functioning after the sympathetic system acts.

Glossary

B

Bargraph A visual representation of data in the form of bars on a graph whose height is a function of the value ascribed to each bar or discrete category. A space is kept between each bar, but if the bars represent a continuous variable rather than discrete categories, the bars may be contiguous and are then known as histograms.

Between subjects design See *within subjects design*.

Binocular cells Those neural cells in the visual area of the brain, the striate cortex, which receive an input from both eyes and which are therefore implicated in the provision of three-dimensional vision (stereopsis). Other cells are driven, that is receive their input only from one eye and are therefore termed monocular cells.

Bit The unit of measurement of information that represents the minimum number of alternatives that can be eliminated i.e. by choosing one of two equally likely alternatives. This may be viewed as the unit $\log^2$.

Buffer store Another term for sensory memory stores in which incoming information is held for very brief periods while they are waiting to receive further processing.

C

Ceiling effect A measurement problem in an experimental design where there is not sufficient range of measurement available with the chosen dependent variable, such that it is very difficult to differentiate amongst the subjects as they are all obtaining high scores. Subjects reach the measurement "ceiling" too easily. See also *floor effect*.

Chronic Persistent, lasting a long time, as opposed to acute.

Classical conditioning Sometimes known as Pavlovian conditioning, this is a process of pairing a neutral stimulus with a reflex-inducing stimulus (the unconditioned stimulus) until by association, the neutral stimulus comes to elicit the reflex-response (the unconditioned response) on its own. The neutral stimulus becomes the conditioned stimulus and the response elicited by it, the conditioned response.

Code The form in which information is held in memory. The nature of the code normally varies from stage to stage (or process to process) in memory, e.g. verbal information is normally entered into STM in an acoustic code (sound pattern code) whether it is presented visually or aurally. Other possible codes include visual, kinaesthetic and semantic codes.

Colour constancy See *perceptual constancy*.

Conditions See *independent variable*.

Control This refers to the necessity to prevent the intrusion of extraneous factors into an experimental design. Such relevant variables will distort the experimental situation which is designed to highlight the effect of one or more independent variables on one or more dependent variables. Control can be achieved using techniques such as randomization, matching and by holding the relevant variable constant. One of the most commonly met relevant variables is the effect of practice.

Control group A group of subjects in a between subjects design of experiment who are as similar as possible to the experimental group or treatment group, but who do not receive the treatment or manipulation of an independent variable.

Corpus callosum The band of nerve fibres that joins together the two halves of the brain and which is severed in split-brain surgery.

Correlated t-test **See** *paired t-test*.

Correlation coefficient (r) This is a measure of the degree of association between any two variables, taking any value between -1 and +1. A relationship indicated by r=0 indicates no association, while an r value of r=1 indicates a perfect relationship so that as one factor gets larger, e.g. height, so does the other, e.g. breadth. A negative value of r indicates that as one factor gets larger so the other gets smaller. There are a number of correlation statistics, each of which makes different assumptions about the data, such as Pearson's Product-moment and Spearman's Rank Order Correlation.

Contextual facilitation The simplification of a processing task due to the context within which the target is placed. Thus it is easier to process a letter stimulus when placed in an alphabetic context than when placed in a numeric context. In a similar way, it is easier to recognize the milkman's face when he appears at your front door with a milk bottle than when he appears in the swimming pool at your holiday hotel.

Counterbalance A technique used in experimental design to control for order or carry-over effects in testing. These effects result from within subjects designs where each subject is tested in each of the experimental conditions and carrying out one part of the experiment will affect carrying out a subsequent part of the experiment. There are a number of counterbalancing techniques, but all attempt to minimize the sequencing problem by having each of the conditions appear equally often in each possible position in the sequence. This can be done within an individual subject or across subjects. For example, if each subject has to do tasks A and B, the experimenter could give task A then B, and then reverse the order and give the tasks again, as B then A, making an A B B A design. The usual guide is to give each condition a number equivalent to the locations it takes up in testing, add these numbers together and ensure that they are equal for all conditions, e.g. A takes positions 1 and 4 = 5, and B takes positions 2 and 3 = 5. Further control can be obtained by giving half the subjects the alternative ordering - B A A B, which helps control for nonlinear order effects.

CVC trigrams Triplets of letters used as stimuli in memory experiments. They take the form Consonant-Vowel-Consonant and are meant to be syllables that are meaningless, i.e. nonsense syllables, for example GUK.

D

Dark adaptation The process by which the eye regains its maximum sensitivity to light when placed in darkness for about 15 minutes. The cones adapt faster than the rods, but never attain the same absolute level of sensitivity.

Debriefing The procedure by which a subject is informed about the experiment in which he has just been a subject. This is important because by their very nature, psychology experiments may often not work out if subjects know in advance what is expected of them, or may work too well because of subject bias. As a result subjects are rarely told the full details of an experiment in advance. It is therefore ethically necessary to give them a full debriefing and this will also help the public relations side of experimental psychology. An additional benefit of debriefing is that you can obtain details of the subject's own experience of the study which may be very helpful in showing up faults in your experiment or suggesting additional aspects to explore.

Decay The fading of information from a memory store as a result of the passage of time. It is suggested as an important reason for memory loss in sensory memory, less so in STM and even less in LTM.

Declarative Referring to that part of the memory system which is specifically concerned with the encoding, storage and retrieval of factual information, e.g. your date-of-birth, or what your bank manager looks like.

Degrees of freedom A value used to assist in determining the probability of obtaining a given test statistic such as the t-value (i.e. the level of significance). The reason for using degrees of freedom (df) is that the more subjects that are tested, the more likely it is that the distribution of experimental results is a truly random one. The result of this is that a more conservative value of the test statistic can be accepted when the number of subjects is large. Degrees of freedom are calculated from the number of subjects in an experiment or in a condition of an experiment, or sometimes from the number of conditions in an experiment (e.g. when using the ANOVA test). Normally the actual value of df is one less than the number of subjects or conditions. The reason for this is that the last value

Glossary

can always be predicted from the other values. Imagine that you have 10 pegs to locate in 10 holes in a board. Positioning the first 9 always gives you some choice or freedom in placement, while with the last peg you have no freedom at all, since only one place remains.

Dependent variable The dependent variable is that response of the subject which is measured by the experimenter to see if it changes in a systematic way as the independent variable is introduced. For example, what is the effect of noise (the independent variable) on performing mental arithmetic (the dependent variable).

Difference threshold The smallest detectable change in a physical stimulus. Sometimes called a JND or just noticeable difference.

E

Electroencephalogram The EEG is a record of the electrical activity of the brain.

Eidetic imagery Also known as photographic memory, this involves the storing of visual input in a visual code that is so detailed that it can be scanned as if the original was still being viewed. It is very rare, particularly after childhood has been passed.

Endocrine system Glands which are specialized for the production of hormonal substances.

Epilepsy A clinical condition caused by a chronic functional impairment of the central nervous system, which is associated with sudden losses of consciousness and even convulsive seizures caused by massive generalized firing of brain cells. Its treatment may involve severing the corpus callosum to prevent the spread of neural firing passing from one hemisphere to another.

Epiphenomenon A process or event which is a by-product of another event or process and which is not functionally significant.

Error rate The proportion of errors out of the total number of possible responses made by a subject in an experiment. It is usually expressed as a percentage or as a fraction e.g. If a subject makes 15 mistakes in 75 trials, his error rate can be expressed as 0.2 or 20%.

Experimental group This is a group of subjects who receive a specific experimental condition which is different from that received by any other group. The conditions received by these groups make up the different levels of an independent variable or factor or indeed combinations of levels of two or more factors.

Experimental hypothesis This is a concise statement of the predictions made by the experimenter about the effects he expects to find from his experimental manipulations and these should ideally be based on theoretical argument or past experience. Its converse is the null hypothesis.

Experimenter effect An effect which can intrude as an unwanted variable in many experiments in which the subjects are unwittingly influenced by the experimenter to behave or respond in ways that the experimenter wants. This can result from the subject trying to please the experimenter, but it can also happen with animals such as rats. In this type of situation, it is the experimenter's preconceptions which usually act to alter his behaviour towards the subject animals or his perception of their behaviour. Thus an experimenter who is told that he is testing a very stupid strain of rats will often report that they learn more slowly than will an experimenter told that the same group of rats is a particularly bright one. See also response bias.

F

Facilitation Making performance on task B easier because of performance on task A. See also *interference*.

Factors See *independent variable*.

Fatigue effect See *practice effect*.

Feedback Knowledge of results, information that allows the modification of ongoing responses i.e. learning, and which frequently improves motivation on experimental tasks.

Fixation A single look with the eye or eyes.

Fixation spot A mark, such as a cross, on a stimulus display on which the subject is to fixate in order to control for the effect of eye movements or to direct his attention to a specific target.

Floor effect A measurement problem in an experimental design where there is not sufficient range of measurement available with the chosen dependent variable, such that it is very difficult to differentiate amongst the subjects as they are all obtaining low scores. Subjects reach the measurement "floor" too easily. See also *ceiling effect*.

Fovea That small central part of the retina which forms a pit in which is concentrated the greatest density of cones and no rods. As a result it provides the sharpest, most detailed vision of any part of the retina. See also periphery.

Frequency distribution This is obtained by classifying a set of measurements into different classes (.g. 10-19, 20-29....) and noting the frequency with which the measurements fall into each class. When graphed as a frequency histogram, the class intervals are usually plotted on the horizontal (X) axis and frequency on the vertical (Y) axis.

G

Galvanic skin response The GSR is a record of the electrical conductivity of the surface of the skin.

General Adaptation Syndrome The three-stage reaction of the body to stress described by Selye, which consists of the alarm reaction, resistance and exhaustion stages.

H

Histogram See *bar graph*.

Homograph A form of spelling which has multiple meanings, for example "might".

Hormones Chemical substances produced by endocrine glands within the body that affect specific functions (such as growth) at different parts of the body usually after travelling through the blood.

Hypothalamus A part of the forebrain which is implicated in the control of certain autonomic nervous system functions such as sleep, temperature control and appetite.

Hypothesis A provisional statement about the relationship between one or more independent variables and one or more dependent variables. This is the first stage in the operation of the experimental method. The hypothesis may be one-tailed or two-tailed. This implies that the hypothesis may specify the direction of the effect, e.g. "appropriate context makes recognition of a stimulus faster" or it may not specify the direction of the effect, e.g. "familiarity with a word will affect the strength of memory for that word when it appears in a word list". This has implications for the statistical test used to examine the resulting data since there is obviously twice the probability of getting some purely chance effect when the direction of the expected effect is not specified and could occur in either of two directions. Therefore when looking up statistical tables to determine the probability of obtaining a value of a statistic by chance, you need to select the appropriate level of significance – one-tailed or two-tailed.

I

Icon The internal visual code or representation of a visual input.

Glossary

Iconic memory The sensory memory store that maintains visual input for a brief period before further coding takes place in memory or the information is lost by decay or interference.

Illusion The non-veridical perception that arises from a particular sensory input. Also used to refer to the illusion provoking stimulus itself.

Imagery Mental pictures which represent sensory experience, usually visual.

Immune system The body system which is specialized in providing resistance to invading organisms such as bacteria and viruses.

Independent variable The purpose of the experiment is to assess the effects of one or more independent variables on the dependent variable/s. The independent variable is often referred to as a factor and the different values of the factor are called levels of that factor. For example, the factor "size of stimulus" could have three different levels – small, medium and large. Each different set of circumstances in which a sample of subjects is run is known as a condition of the experiment.

Independent t-test A statistical test of the difference between two samples obtained from independent groups. It tests the null hypothesis that the two populations have the same mean. It is a parametric test and must satisfy the requirements of such tests as far as the data are concerned. See *paired t-test*.

Inferior colliculus That part of the mid-brain which is involved in processing and relaying auditory information. See also *superior colliculus*.

Information That which allows a choice between alternatives, reducing uncertainty. It is measured in *bits*.

Information processing That model of the human cognitive system which views the brain as a processor of information which flows through the brain while a variety of operations are performed upon it.

Interaction This refers to the situation in multi-factor experiments where there is an effect on the dependent variable of one factor, but only with certain levels of another factor. Thus noise may have a deleterious effect on mental arithmetic performance only when the subject is tired and not when he is rested. The best way to see if an interaction exists is to draw a graph of the factors concerned and statistical tests can then be performed. The ANOVA indicates interactions during its calculation. No significant main effect can be interpreted by itself if it is also included in a significant interaction.

Interference Generally the process by which performing one task can lead to poorer performance on another. More specifically, in the context of memory research, the loss of memory due to prior learning interfering with or inhibiting later learning (proactive), or due to new learning interfering with prior learning (retroactive).

Inter-ocular transfer A situation in which the input to one eye influences the operation of the other eye which has never directly experienced the first eye's stimulus.

Isomorphic Having close similarity, but in unrelated forms; particularly in terms of the interrelationships between the parts.

L

Levels See *independent variable*.

Lexical decision task The LDT is a task in which the subject is required to decide whether a sequence of letters is or is not a valid word.

Lexicon The mental dictionary of words (semantic memory).

Linear A unidimensional relationship between two variables that can be described by a straight line function on a graph.

Line graph A graph in which those plotted values which are related, are connected by lines. See also *bar graph*.

Location constancy See *perceptual constancy*.

M

Main effect A term used to refer to an independent variable and which appears in statistical discussions as a "significant or (non-significant) main effect". This implies that the independent variable in question had (or did not have) a reliable effect on the measured dependent variable, but see *interaction*.

Matched-pairs t-test See *paired t-test*.

Matrix A rectangular array of items (usually numbers) arranged in ordered rows and columns.

Mean This is a summary statistic which may take several forms. The Arithmetic mean is a measure of the average value of a set of measurements and is calculated by adding together all the values and dividing this total by the number of values, i.e. the sample size. Its particular strength is that it takes into account all the data in a set. The geometric mean and the harmonic mean are not often met in psychological statistics. See *median* and *mode*.

Meaningfulness The number of associations typically made with a given word, e.g. it is possible to make many associations with the word "house" (garden, roof, chair etc), but few associations can be made with "grommet".

Measure of central tendency See *mean*, *median* and *mode*.

Median A measure of the average of a set of values calculated as the middle value where the sample size is uneven, or as the arithmetic mean of the two middle values if the sample size is an even number. Its usefulness lies in its relative insensitivity to extreme values or outliers such as one might find with reaction time data where a subject may press a key too soon by accident thus getting a very short time, or he may have a lapse of concentration and obtain an extremely long time. See *mean* and *mode*.

Mental chronometry The study of the time course of information flow through the human nervous system.

Method of adjustment A psychophysical procedure which involves the subject actively changing the value of a variable until, for example, he judges it to be equal to a standard value. Generally the procedure is carried out in both directions, increasing the value of the variable from a starting value below the standard and decreasing the value of the variable from a starting value above the standard.

Microelectrodes Miniature metal conductors which are used to pick up the electrical activity of single nerve cells within the brain. They generally take the form of a very fine needle with two conducting surfaces and they are implanted through a hole drilled in the skull into the desired location in the brain. This location is identified by means of a stereotaxic instrument (a sophisticated kind of head clamp) and stereotaxic maps, which are sets of reference coordinates locating parts of the brain in three-dimensions.

Mid-brain The middle part of the brain below the neocortex which contains structures such as the superior colliculus and the inferior colliculus.

Mixed design See *within subjects design*.

Mode The most frequently occurring value in a set of values.

Monocular cells See *binocular cells*.

Monocular viewing Looking at a stimulus with only one eye.

Glossary

Msec A millisecond; a measure of time in units of 1/1000 of a second.

Multiple t-tests See *a priori*.

Multiple regression A statistical technique which can be used to predict values of a dependent variable from prior knowledge about the values of related variables. The method is frequently used to determine the order of importance of a set of variables in explaining the variance in a set of data.

N

Negative after-effects See *adaptation*.

Negative skew See *skew*.

Neuroelectrophysiological recording The process by which the electrical activity of nerve cells is recorded and measured.

Neurons Specialized cells which consist of a cell body with dendrites and an axon at the end of which are terminal buttons which link electrochemically with (synapse with) other nerve cells as well as with gland cells and muscle fibers. The complex integration of neurons comprises the nervous system.

Nonsense syllables See *CVC trigrams*.

Norms A set of authoritative standards concerning a particular factor or factors. For example, the set of norms which indicate age-appropriate behaviour for children as they develop.

Normal distribution More properly termed the normal probability curve, this refers to a "bell-shaped" distribution of scores that is symmetrical about the mean and is typical of the frequency distribution of many psychological variables. The mean, median and mode are equal in this situation.

Null hypothesis A statement which indicates that there is no effect of one variable upon another. For example, if the experimental hypothesis is that "we expect that high levels of noise will have a larger detrimental effect on mental arithmetic performance than low levels of noise" then the null hypothesis would be that "there is no difference in the mental arithmetic performance of two groups, one of whom has received high levels of noise and the other has received low levels of noise". A statistical test is normally used to test the null hypothesis and to reject it only if there is at best a 5 in 100 (5%) chance of the reported difference in mental arithmetic scores occurring by chance. Remember that an experimental hypothesis can never be proved, the null hypothesis has to be disproved.

O

One-tailed test See *hypothesis*

Operational definitions Those definitions of an experimental measure or manipulation which are couched in terms of the actual operations carried out by the experimenter in measuring or manipulating them.

Order effect The influence on a subject's response measures of being involved in more than one condition of an experiment. For example, a subject could be asked to learn a set of words in one condition and to learn a different set in a second condition. There could be some transfer effect across conditions such that being a subject in the first condition improves or makes worse his performance in the second condition. A between subjects design is to be preferred where order effects are expected, or counterbalancing should be instituted. See also facilitation and interference.

Origin The point of intersection of the two axes (the vertical ordinate – and the horizontal abscissa) of a graph.

P

Paired comparisons test See *a priori* and *a posteriori*.

Paired t-test Sometimes known as a matched pairs or a correlated t-test, this statistical test examines the null hypothesis that the mean difference between pairs of scores is zero. It looks at the differences between pairs of scores that have been obtained from the same subject at different times or have been obtained from different subjects that have been considered equivalent or matched on the basis of a variable that has a known relationship to the independent variable being assessed. It is a parametric test and must satisfy the appropriate requirements as far as data are concerned.

Paradigm Another term for experimental method.

Parametric Refers to statistical tests that can be used with parametric data. Such data must satisfy certain strict assumptions. Each sample of data must be drawn from a normally distributed population, each of the populations must have the same variance and the data must be measurable on an interval scale, i.e. where the points of measurement can be ordered along a dimension and the distance between points on the dimension can be specified. Median reaction time data, for example, will usually satisfy these criteria. Where the assumptions about population measures cannot be upheld, non-parametric tests which make fewer assumptions can be employed.

Perception The further processing of sensations to supply a meaningful analysis based on prior experience and world knowledge. For example the experience of a tinkling, brass bell as an object, rather than as a tone and a patch of the colour gold. See also sensation.

Perceptual confusion A situation where one percept or perceptual recognition is confused with or mistaken for another.

Perceptual constancy The world is by-and-large a stable one of relatively unchanging objects. As a result, the visual system makes use of this to ensure veridical perception. Thus, while objects produce retinal images of quite different sizes at different distances from the eyes, they tend to be seen as fairly constant in size. In the same way, the visual system interprets colour, shape and location information as being more constant than the actual sensory experience really is.

Perceptual defence The reduction in the ability to perceive stimuli which have adverse emotional associations.

Periphery The outer region of the retina which contains mainly rods and few cones. The packing density is low and the degree of acuity or sharpness of vision is fairly poor. Colour vision is also very limited. See also *fovea*.

Phonemes The smallest units of sound which can be meaningfully distinguished from other units within a given language.

Pilot study A preliminary investigation to determine the practicality of a piece of research, to validate the procedure and to establish the possible operation of any relevant variables.

Pituitary gland A gland which is attached to the hypothalamus and is part of the endocrine system

Population The complete set of subjects or of measures from all subjects with which the experimenter is concerned, e.g. all first year psychology students in the University of Glasgow. See sample *size*.

Positron Emission Tomography A technique in which a subject is given a dose of a radioactively labeled compound such as glucose, which is then taken up through the metabolic process by those cells in the brain which are currently active. Indeed the more active the cells, the more the radioactive pick-up and the subsequent emission of positrons which act to create gamma rays. It is these gamma rays which are then detected by monitors scanning the brain and which are mapped by computer analysis to produce a picture of the brain.

Power The power of a statistical test refers to the test's sensitivity, that is, the extent to which it is likely to pinpoint real differences which exist within the data.

Glossary

Practice effect A situation where performance in an experiment improves with experience over time. It might be counteracted eventually by a fatigue effect where performance would tend to decrease over time as physical tiredness increases and motivation perhaps declines. See *counterbalance*.

Precognition Knowledge about an event in advance of its occurrence which has been obtained through psychic transmission.

Proactive interference See *interference*.

Probability The chance of an event occurring, on a scale form 0 to 1, where 0 represents no chance of an event occurring and 1 represents certainty that the event will occur. The term is used in statistical testing where the probability of obtaining a particular value of the test statistic is assessed. If that probability is less than 0.05 then the event is usually assumed to be unlikely to have occurred by chance. See also *significance*.

Procedural Referring to that part of the memory system which is specifically concerned with the encoding, storage and retrieval of programs for skills, e.g. squaring a given number or driving a car.

Pronounceableness The relative ease with which a word can be pronounced in speech by the average person. For example, "grate" is more easily pronounced than "fauna".

Pre-attentive processes Processes which take place at an unconscious level and which may guide the focus of conscious attention in functionally appropriate ways.

Prime A word that when it appears, prepares or readies the system for processing a later word.

Psychophysics The physics of mental experience, involving the scientific measurement of the relationship between physical values of stimulation and their sensory and perceptual equivalents.

Psychophysiology The branch of psychology which measures physiological indices such as heart rate and skin conductance and infers changes in mental states such as emotions from these indices.

Psychokinesis The ability to use mental energy to move physical objects at a distance.

R

Random A mathematical concept referring to the equal likelihood of selection of any item in a set of items. Randomization techniques are often used in experiments to ensure that there is no systematic bias in the selection of subjects, of stimuli or of conditions in an experiment. Tables of random numbers can be used or a mathematical procedure adopted as is done by computer systems. Remember that random number tables cease to be random if you always start at the same point and proceed in the same sequence or if a computer always uses the same start number or "seed" for its calculations, as most home computers actually do.

Random mask See *visual mask*.

Range This assesses the spread of variability of a set of measures, being the difference between the largest and the smallest value. More accurately it is the largest value minus the smallest plus 1 to allow for the exact limits of the two extreme scores in the range. In the series 20, 25, 29, 37, 42, 56, 58, the range is 58 minus 20 inches, plus 1, i.e. 39 inches. Quite commonly, the extreme scores are simply presented as follows: "the range = 20-58 inches" rather than as a single figure. The range is of limited usefulness as it tells us nothing about the distribution of scores within these limits.

Receiver-operating characteristics (ROC) Also called the Relative operating characteristic, provides a graphical representation of the relationship between "hits" and "false alarms" under different conditions of stimulus probability or payoff, where the experimental manipulations lead the subject to alter his criterion of judgment to generate successive points on the graph.

Relevant variable See *control*.

Repeated measures See *Analysis of Variance*.

Response bias A tendency for the subject to respond more in one way than another in an experiment. This is an extraneous influence in a study which will make it harder to discern the effect of the independent variable. It often results from the way that the subject construes or interprets the experiment.

Response contingency In psychological experiments the subjects is usually assumed to operate in a uniform way over time, showing only minor variations about a mean level of performance. In reality, subjects demonstrate marked influence by their immediate setting and are affected by the contingencies associated with their responses. For example, if there are important consequences for a given response -such as detecting a blip on a radar screen this will affect a subject's judgment. This si particularly important in psychophysics and in signal detection theory.

Response facilitation A process of making it easier to produce a particular response at the expense of other possible responses.

Retina The layer of light-sensitive cells at the back of the eye which receives light focused by the lens onto rod and cone cells. These receptor cells change the light energy into electrical energy through an electrochemical bleaching process and this electrical activity is passed on to the visual areas within the brain (lateral geniculate nucleus, superior colliculus and striate cortex).

Retroactive interference See *interference*.

Rote rehearsal The process of memorization of material by continuous repetition. Often known as primary or surface rehearsal.

S

Saccade Rapid, short eye movement which takes the eyes from one feature to another in a stimulus display.

Sacrificed The euphemistic term for killing an experimental animal after its experimental usefulness is over, or in situations where an examination of internal systems, such as parts of the brain, is required.

Sample size The number of subjects in the subset of subjects (or of the measurements of subjects) that has been selected from the study population. The derived sample statistics provide estimates of the population statistics.

Scattergram A graph on which are plotted a "scatter" of points, each of which represents a value of the variable A (on the Y-axis or ordinate) and of the variable B (on the X-axis or abscissa). This is commonly used in correlational research where there may be a score on two tests for each subject in the study and a graphical representation of the relationship between the two sets of test scores is required. As an example, a correlation coefficient of r=1 would show on the graph as a perfect straight line sloping upwards from left to right at 45 degrees to the axes. Low scores are associated with low scores and high scores with high scores.

Sensation The primary experience of stimuli provided through the operation of the sensory systems. For example, the experience of a tone or a patch of gold colour. See also *perception*.

Shape constancy See *perceptual constancy*.

Signal detection theory A theory of stimulus detection which assumes that to detect a sensory event involves a discrimination between signal (the stimulus) and noise (the background). The detectability of a signal is considered to be a probabilistic event which can be measured by the relative proportion of "hits", "misses", "correct negatives" and "false alarms". See also *receiver-operating characteristics*. Two measures can be produced:

d' (d prime) which indicates the sensitivity of the system

β (Beta) which indicates the nature of the response criterion adopted (cautious or lax).

Glossary

Significance The result of any statistical test is said to be significant and the null hypothesis overturned if the outcome of the test, e.g the t value, is sufficiently unlikely to have occurred by chance as there is less than a 5 in 100 chance of it occurring. A more stringent test would only accept the 1% level of significance, i.e. the obtained statistic would only be found to occur by chance on 1 occasion in 100. See also *probability*.

Simple effects See *a priori* and *a posteriori*.

Size constancy See *perceptual constancy*.

Skew A departure from a symmetrical, normal distribution where there is either a long tail to the left (negative skew), found for example where most students perform reasonably in an exam and a few do very badly; or there is a long tail to the right (positive skew), found for example when most perform reasonably and a few do very well. The degree of skew in a distribution may be assessed by subtracting the mode from the mean and dividing the result by the standard deviation. A symmetrical distribution will give a skew value of zero, a positive skew will be shown by a positive value and a negative skew by a negative value.

Spearman's Rank Order Correlation See *correlation coefficient*.

Speed-accuracy trade-off An inverse relationship exists between speed and accuracy such that concentrating on speed reduces accuracy and vice versa. This indicates a fundamental characteristic of the way that much of our processing systems such as the pattern recognition system work.

Split-brain A condition in which a human or animal has had the corpus callosum surgically cut in order to prevent direct communication between the two hemispheres of the brain.

Standard deviation The square root of the variance.

Stress A physiological state of hormonal and physiological changes associated with disruptive circumstances such as those involving conflict.

Subception Discrimination without conscious awareness.

Subvocalization Refers to implicit speech, silent, inward directed speech, as in the soundless rehearsal of a word list.

Superior colliculus That part of the mid-brain which is involved in the processing and relaying of visual information. Identification of spatial location and the control of eye-movements are possible functions of this area. See also inferior colliculus.

Suprathreshold Above *threshold*.

T

Tachistoscope A device which allows the controlled presentation of a visual stimulus for very brief durations. More complex instruments allow a sequence of stimuli to be shown where the duration of the presentation of each is programmed as are the intervals between the stimuli.

Template An internal model or representation, a kind of miniature copy.

T-test See *paired t-test* and *independent t-test*.

Threshold A boundary between the perceptible and the imperceptible. Usually that value of a variable stimulus that can be detected on 5 % of its occurrences is said to be the threshold value. There are various types of threshold, see absolute threshold and difference threshold.

Two-tailed test See *hypothesis*.

V

Variance A measure of the distribution or spread of scores in a set of data. This assessment of variability is calculated by summing the squares of the deviations of each score from the mean of the scores and dividing the obtained result by the sample size minus 1. It is the same as the square of the standard deviation.

Verbal shadowing Shadowing is an experimental technique used in the study of selective attention in which a passage of text is presented to a subject whose task is to repeat the text simultaneously, usually out loud. The complication arises when a competing passage is presented at the same time and the amount and type of errors produced can provide valuable information about attention. There are two forms–auditory, where one passage is usually played on a tape-recorder through headphones into one ear while the second passage is played through the other ear, the subject's task being to repeat only the message in a preselected ear; and verbal, where the two passages are printed with the lines in an interleaved fashion on a page. The subjects task is to read only every alternate line.

Visual angle A convenient means of specifying the size and distance of a visual stimulus in degrees and minutes of arc. The visual angle subtended by a stimulus (i.e. the angle it is opposite to) is defined by the following formula, where h is the size of the stimulus and d is the distance from the subject's eye:

$$X° = (\arctan (h / (2 \times d))) \times 2$$

This formula is illustrated in the following diagram:

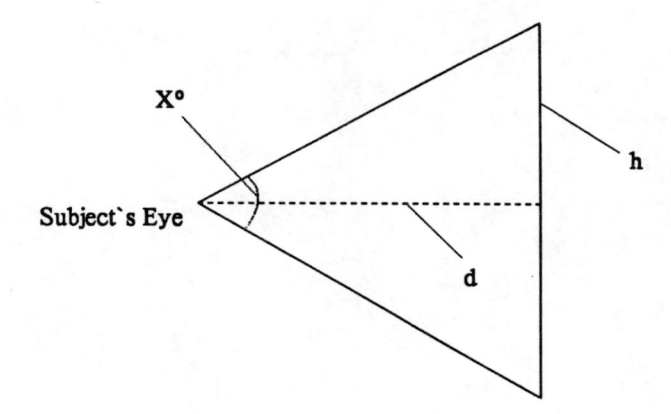

Visual mask A random array of visual shapes, dots lines etc. which is presented after the stimulus in a tachistoscopic experiment in order to mask or wipe out the visual image which would otherwise remain on a computer screen because of the slow decay rate of the screen phosphors or remain on the retina in the form of an after-image. Masks overcome the phenomenon of visual persistence in which a visual image tends to last for longer than the duration of the exposure time. The effect of this is to prolong the time that the stimulus in the form of an icon can be viewed. The mask ensures that the icon is removed and therefore cannot influence the task being examined.

Visual persistence See *visual mask*.

Visual search A process by which we scan our environment to locate a specific target.

Glossary

Vividness The clarity or strength of a mental image.

W

Within subjects design An experimental design in which every subject is presented with every possible combination of the independent variables, as opposed to a between subjects design in which each subject is used in only one condition and different groups therefore make up the different conditions. A mixture of the two is also possible and this is called a mixed design.

Notes

Notes

RECORD SHEET of _____

	Experimental Chapter	Tutor's Signature

Chapter 1:   Simple Reaction Time   _____

Comments _____

_____

Chapter 2:   Word Frequency and Recognition Speed   _____

Comments _____

_____

Chapter 3:   Waterfall Effect   _____

Comments _____

_____

Chapter 4:   Muller–Lyer Illusion   _____

Comments _____

_____

Chapter 5:   Prisoner's Dilemma   _____

Comments _____

_____

Chapter 6:   Extra-sensory Perception (ESP)   _____

Comments _____

_____

Chapter 7:   Mental Imagery I and II   _____

Comments _____

_____

Chapter 8: Reading and Selective Attention _____

Comments _____
_____

Chapter 9: Stress, Life Events and Personality Type _____

Comments _____
_____

Chapter 10: Hemispheric Asymmetry I and II _____

Comments _____
_____

Chapter 11: Subliminal Perception _____

Comments _____
_____